DEPARTMENT OF THE NAVY
HEADQUARTERS UNITED STATES MARINE CORPS
3000 MARINE CORPS PENTAGON
WASHINGTON, DC 20350-3000

I0425953

C-9B TRAINING AND READINESS (T&R) MANUAL

DEPARTMENT OF THE NAVY
HEADQUARTERS UNITED STATES MARINE CORPS
3000 MARINE CORPS PENTAGON
WASHINGTON, DC 20350-3000

NAVMC 3500.31A
C4610
22 NOV 2011

NAVMC 3500.31A

From: Commandant of the Marine Corps
To: Distribution List

Subj: C-9B TRAINING AND READINESS (T&R) MANUAL

Ref: (a) NAVMC 3500.14C

Encl: (1) C-9B T&R MANUAL

1. Purpose. To revise standards and regulations regarding the training of C-9B aircrew per the reference.

2. Cancellation. NAVMC 3500.31.

3. Scope. Significant changes include:

    a. Mission Essential Task (MET) incorporation to facilitate MET-based readiness.

    b. Incorporation of Marine Corps Task (MCT) list.

    c. Addition of Aviation Career Progression Model (ACPM) training requirements.

    d. Emphasis on mission skills versus core skills to support MET-based reporting.

    e. Re-naming and re-numbering of phases from 3-digit to 4-digit codes.

4. Information. Recommended changes to this Manual are invited and may be submitted via the syllabus sponsor and the appropriate chain of command to: Commanding General (CG), Training and Education Command (TECOM), Aviation Training Division (ATD) using standard naval correspondence or the Automated Message Handling System (AMHS) plain language address: CG TECOM ATD.

5. Command. This Manual is applicable to the Marine Corps Total Force.

6. Certification. Reviewed and approved this date.

R. C. FOX
By direction

DISTRIBUTION: PCN 10033196800

DISTRIBUTION STATEMENT A: Approved for public release; distribution is unlimited.

CHAPTER 1

C-9B

CHAPTER 1

C-9B UNIT

1.0   TRAINING AND READINESS REQUIREMENTS. The Marine Aviation Training and Readiness (T&R) Program provides the Marine Air-Ground Task Force (MAGTF) commander with an Aviation Combat Element (ACE) capable of executing the six functions of Marine Aviation. The T&R Program is the fundamental tool used by commanders to construct, attain, and maintain effective training programs. The standards established in this program are validated by subject matter experts to maximize combat capabilities for assigned METs while conserving resources. These standards describe and define unit capabilities and requirements necessary to maintain proficiency in mission skills and combat leadership. Training events are based on specific requirements and performance standards to ensure a common base of training and depth of combat capability.

1.1   MISSION. The primary mission of the C-9B is to support the MAGTF Commander by providing time sensitive air transport of routine and high priority passengers and cargo as tasked by Headquarters Marine Corps Aviation Manpower and Support Branch (ASM) or the Joint Operational Support Airlift Center (JOSAC).

1.2   TABLE OF ORGANIZATION (T/O). Communities with more than one T/O will provide a table for each and note those units and subunits assigned to each.

1.2.1   Table of Organization

VMR-1/C-9B	
T/O M02220	
2 A/C	
Crew Composition	Total(s)
Pilots	4
Augment Pilots	7
Crew Chiefs	8
Loadmasters	5
2nd Loadmaster	0

1.3   SIX FUNCTIONS OF MARINE AVIATION

SIX FUNCTIONS OF MARINE AVIATION		
FUNCTION	ABBREVIATION	DESCRIPTION
Offensive Air Support	OAS	OAS involves air operations that are conducted against enemy installations, facilities, and personnel in order to directly assist in the attainment of MAGTF objectives by destroying enemy resources or isolating enemy military forces. Its primary support of the warfighting functions is to provide fires and force protection through CAS and DAS.
Assault Support	ASPT	ASPT contributes to the warfighting functions of maneuver and logistics. Maneuver warfare demands rapid, flexible maneuverability to achieve a decision. Assault support uses aircraft to provide tactical mobility and logistic support to the MAGTF for the movement of high priority personnel and cargo within the immediate area of operations (or the evacuation of personnel and cargo).
Anti-Air Warfare	AAW	AAW is the actions used to destroy or reduce the enemy air and missile threat to an acceptable level. The primary purpose of AAW is to gain and maintain whatever degree of air superiority is required; this permits the conduct of operations without prohibitive interference by opposing air and missile forces. AAW's other purpose is force protection.
Electronic Warfare	EW	EW is any military action involving the use of electromagnetic and directed energy to control the electromagnetic spectrum or to attack the enemy. EW supports the warfighting functions of fires, command and control, and intelligence through the three major subdivisions: electronic attack, electronic protection, and electronic warfare support.
Control of Aircraft & Missiles	CoA&M	The control of aircraft and missiles supports the warfighting function of Command and Control. The ACE Commander maintains centralized command, while control is decentralized and executed through the Marine Air Command and Control System (MACCS). CoA&M integrates the other five functions of Marine Aviation by providing the commander with the ability to exercise Command and Control authority over Marine Aviation assets.
Aerial Reconnaissance	AerRec	AerRec employs visual observation and/or sensors in aerial vehicles to acquire intelligence information. It supports the intelligence warfighting function and is employed tactically, operationally, and strategically. The three types of air reconnaissance are visual, multi-sensor imagery, and electronic.

1.4   CORE/MISSION/CORE PLUS SKILL ABBREVIATIONS

VMR-1/C-9B	
CORE/MISSION/CORE PLUS SKILL ABBREVIATIONS	
CORE SKILLS (2000 Phase)	
REC SIM	Recurrent Simulator
T2P REV	Transport 2nd Pilot Review
NAV	Navigation
TAC REV	Transport Aircraft Commander Review
RFAM	Review Familiarization
IFAM	International Familiarization
PFAM	Passenger Familiarization
VFAM	Distinguished Visitor Familiarization
HAZFAM	Hazardous Cargo
MISSION SKILLS (3000 Phase)	
ALS	Air Logistics Support
OSA	Operational Support Airlift
CORE PLUS SKILL (4000 Phase)	
IFAM	International Familiarization
MAXCPL	Maximum Cargo and Passenger Loading

1.5   MISSION ESSENTIAL TASK LIST (METL). The unit METL consists of Mission Essential Tasks (METs).

VMR-1/C-9B		
MISSION ESSENTIAL TASK LIST (METL)		
CORE		
MET	ABBREVIATION	MCT DESCRIPTION
MCT 1.3.4.1.2	OSA	Conduct Operational Support Airlift
MCT 4.3.8	ALS	Conduct Air Logistics Support

1.6   MISSION ESSENTIAL TASK (MET) TO SIX FUNCTIONS OF MARINE AVIATION

VMR-1/C-9B							
MISSION ESSENTIAL TASK (MET) TO SIX FUNCTIONS OF MARINE AVIATION							
MET	ABBREVIATION	SIX FUNCTIONS OF MARINE AVIATION					
		OAS	ASPT	AAW	EW	CoA&M	AerRec
MCT 1.3.4.1.2	OSA		X				
MCT 4.3.8	ALS		X				

1.7   MISSION ESSENTIAL TASKS (MET) OUTPUT STANDARDS

1.7.1   Flying Squadrons

VMR-1/C-9B				
CORE MET OUTPUT STANDARDS				
2 Aircraft				
MET	ABBREVIATION	MAXIMUM DAILY SORTIES	MAXIMUM SORTIES PER MET	CMMR (CREWS)
MCT 1.3.4.1.2	OSA	2	2	2
MCT 4.3.8	ALS		2	2

Note: Based on an average sortie duration of 3.5 hrs.

1.8   MET TO CORE/MISSION/CORE PLUS SKILL MATRIX. Provides a pictorial
view of the relationship between the Core MCT (Marine Corps Task) and each
Core/Mission skill required to perform the MCT.

VMR-1/C-9B												
MISSION ESSENTIAL TASK (MET) to CORE/MISSION/CORE PLUS SKILL MATRIX												
Mission Essential Task (MET)	CORE SKILLS (2000 Phase)									MISSION SKILLS (3000 Phase)		CORE PLUS SKILLS (4000 Phase)
	REC SIM	T2P REV	NAV	TAC REV	RFAM	IFAM	PFAM	VFAM	HAZFAM	OSA	ALS	IFAM	MAXCPL
MCT 1.3.4.1.2 (OSA)	X	X	X	X	X	X	X	X	X	X		X	X
MCT 4.3.8 (ALS)	X	X	X	X	X	X	X	X	X		X	X	X

1.9   CMMR CORE/MISSION CREW DEFINITION AND PROFICIENCY REQUIREMENTS
(2000, 3000, and 4000 Phase)

VMR-1/C-9B					
CORE MODEL MINIMUM REQUIREMENTS (CMMR) [T-2]					
CORE/MISSION/CORE PLUS SKILLS CREW POSITION PROFICIENCY REQUIREMENTS 2 Aircraft					
CORE SKILLS (2000 Phase)					
Core Skills	Pilot	CC	LM	2LM	Total Crews
REC SIM	4	2	N/A	N/A	2
T2P REV	2	N/A	N/A	N/A	1
NAV	4	N/A	N/A	N/A	2
TAC REV	2	N/A	N/A	N/A	1
RFAM	N/A	2	N/A	N/A	2
IFAM	N/A	2	0	0	2
PFAM	N/A	N/A	N/A	2	2
VFAM	N/A	N/A	N/A	2	2
HAZFAM	N/A	N/A	2	N/A	2
MISSION SKILLS (3000 Phase)					
Mission Skills	Pilot	CC	LM	2LM	Total Crews
OSA	4	2	2	2	2
ALS	4	2	2	2	2
CORE PLUS SKILL (4000 Phase)					
IFAM	N/A	0	2	2	2
MAXCPL	N/A	N/A	2	N/A	2

1.10   INSTRUCTOR DESIGNATIONS (5000 Phase)

VMR-1/C-9B				
INSTRUCTOR DESIGNATIONS (5000 Phase) CMMR				
INSTRUCTOR DESIGNATIONS	Pilot	CC	LM	2LM
NE*/NI	1	N/A	N/A	N/A
ANI	1	N/A	N/A	N/A
CC NE*/CC NI	N/A	1	N/A	N/A
CC ANI	N/A	2	N/A	N/A
2LM NE*/2LM NI	N/A	N/A	N/A	1
2LM ANI	N/A	N/A	N/A	2
LM NE*/LM NI	N/A	N/A	1	N/A
LM ANI	N/A	N/A	2	N/A
* At the present time VMR-1 is not the Model Manager for the C-9B but should they become the Model Manager the NATOPS Instructor would become the NATOPS Evaluator.				

1.11   REQUIREMENTS, CERTIFICATIONS, QUALIFICATIONS, AND DESIGNATIONS (R, C, Q & D) (6000 Phase)

VMR-1/C-9B				
REQUIREMENTS, CERTIFICATIONS, QUALIFICATIONS, DESIGNATIONS (R,C,Q,D) (6000 Phase) CMMR [T-2]				
2 Aircraft				
R,C,Q,D	Pilot	CC	LM	2LM
T3P	2	N/A	N/A	N/A
T2P	3	N/A	N/A	N/A
TAC	6	N/A	N/A	N/A
CC	N/A	8	N/A	N/A
2LM	N/A	N/A	N/A	6
LM	N/A	N/A	5	N/A
FCP	2	N/A	N/A	N/A
COMBAT/FLIGHT LEADERSHIP				
2 Aircraft (N/A For the C-9B)				

CHAPTER 2

C-9B PILOT/7551

2.0   INDIVIDUAL TRAINING AND READINESS REQUIREMENTS. This T&R syllabus is based on specific goals and performance standards designed to ensure individual proficiency in Core and Mission Skills. The goal of this chapter is to develop individual and unit war fighting capabilities.

2.1   TRAINING PROGRESSION MODEL. This model represents the recommended training progression for the average VMR-1 C-9B pilot. Units should use the model as a guide to generate individual training plans.

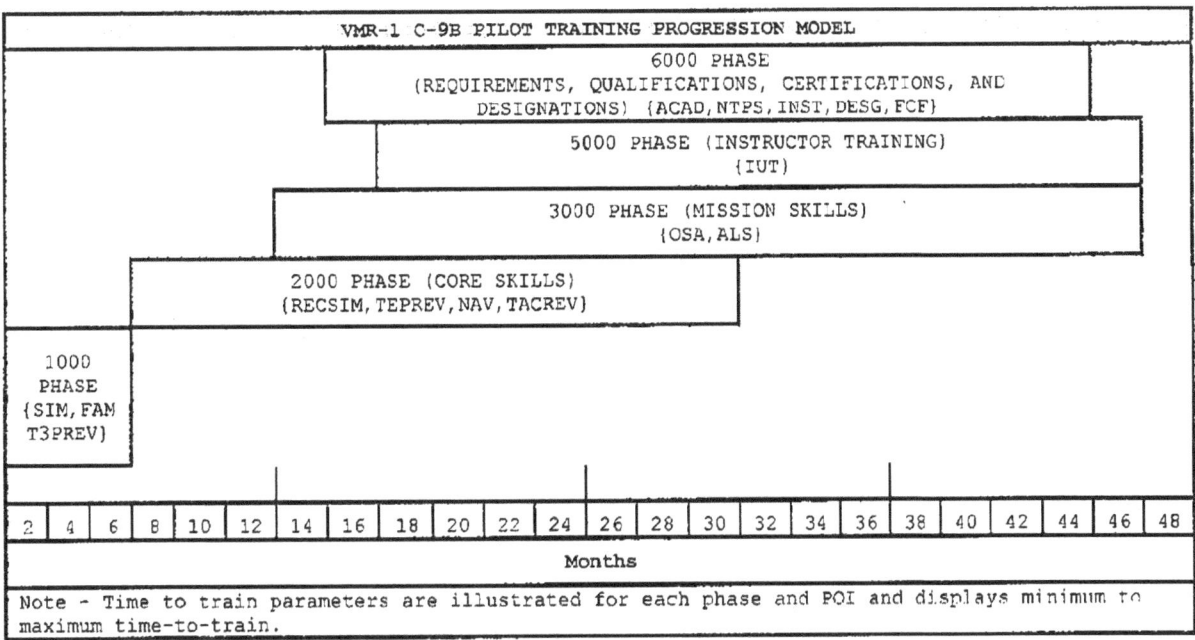

2.2   ABBREVIATIONS

VMR-1 C-9B PILOT	
CORE/MISSION/CORE PLUS SKILL ABBREVIATIONS	
CORE SKILLS (1000 Phase)	
FAM	Familiarization
FBS	Fixed Base Simulator
SIM	Simulator
T3PREV	T3P Review
CORE SKILLS (2000 Phase)	
RECSIM	Recurrent Simulators
T2PREV	T2P Review
NAV	Navigation
TACREV	TAC Review
MISSION SKILLS (3000 Phase)	
OSA	Operational Support Airlift
ALS	Air Logistics Support
INSTRUCTOR (5000 Phase)	
IUT	Instructor Under Training
NI	NATOPS Instructor
ANI	Assistant NATOPS Instructor
NE	NATOPS Evaluator
QUALIFICATIONS AND DESIGNATIONS (6000 Phase)	
ACAD	Academics
NTPS	NATOPS
INST	Instrument
EP	Emergency Procedures
DESG	Designation
FCF	Functional Check Flight

2.3   DEFINITIONS

TERM	DEFINITION
Core Model	The Core Model is the basic foundation or standardized format by which all T&Rs are constructed. The Core Model provides the capability of quantifying both unit and individual training requirements and measuring readiness. This is accomplished by linking community Mission Statements, Mission Essential Task Lists, Output Standards, Core Skill Proficiency Requirements and Combat Leadership Matrices
Core Skill	Fundamental, environmental, or conditional capabilities required to perform basic functions. These basic functions serve as tactical enablers that allow crews to progress to the more complex Mission Skills. Primarily 2000 Phase events but may be introduced in the 1000 Phase.
Mission Skill	Mission Skills enable a unit to execute a specific MET. They are comprised of advanced event(s) that are focused on MET performance and draw upon the knowledge, aeronautical abilities, and situational awareness developed during Core Skill training. 3000 Phase events.
Core Plus Skill	Training events that can be theater specific or that have a low likelihood of occurrence. They may be fundamental, environmental, or conditional capabilities required to perform basic functions. 4000 Phase events.
Core Plus Mission	Training events that can be theater specific or that have a low likelihood of occurrence. They are comprised of advanced event(s) that are focused on Core Plus MET performance and draw upon the knowledge, aeronautical abilities, and situational awareness. 4000 Phase events.
Core Skill Proficiency (CSP)	CSP is a measure of training completion for 2000 Phase events. CSP is attained by executing all events listed in the Attain Table for each Core Skill. The individual must be simultaneously proficient in all events within that Core Skill to attain CSP.
Mission Skill Proficiency (MSP)	MSP is a measure of training completion for 3000 Phase events. MSP is attained by executing all events listed in the Attain Table for each Mission Skill. The individual must be simultaneously proficient in all events within that Mission Skill to attain MSP. MSP is directly related to Training Readiness.
Core Plus Skill Proficiency (CPSP)	CPSP is a measure of training completion for 4000 Phase "Skill" events. CPSP is attained by executing all events listed in the Attain Table for each Core Plus Skill. The individual must be simultaneously proficient in all events within that Core Plus Skill to attain CPSP
Core Plus Mission Proficiency (CPMP)	CPMP is a measure of training completion for 4000 Phase "Mission" events. CPMP is attained by executing all events listed in the Attain Table for each Core Plus Mission. The individual must be simultaneously proficient in all events within that Core Plus Mission to attain CPMP

2.4   INDIVIDUAL CORE/MISSION SKILL PROFICIENCY REQUIREMENTS

2.4.1   Management of individual CSP/MSP serves as the foundation for developing proficiency requirements in DRRS.

2.4.2   Individual CSP is a "Yes/No" status assigned to an individual by Core Skill. When an individual attains and maintains CSP in a Core Skill, the individual counts towards CMMR Unit CSP requirements for that Core Skill.

2.4.3   Proficiency is attained by individual Core/Mission Skill and the training events to be executed within that skill set are determined by POI assignment (Basic or Refresher).

2.4.4   Once proficiency has been attained by Core/Mission Skill (by any POI assignment) then the individual maintains proficiency by executing those events within the maintain column. An individual maintains proficiency by individual Core/Mission Skill.

Note
Individuals may be attaining proficiency
in some Core/Mission/Core Plus Skills
while maintaining proficiency in other
Core/Mission/Core Plus Skills.

2.4.5   Once proficiency has been attained, should one lose proficiency in
an event in the maintain column, proficiency can be attained by demonstrating
proficiency in the event which was delinquent. Should an individual lose
proficiency in all events in the maintain column by Core/Mission Skill, the
individual will be assigned to the Refresher POI for that Core/Mission Skill.
To regain proficiency for that Core/Mission Skill the individual must
demonstrate proficiency in all R-coded events for that Core/Mission Skill.

VMR-1 C-9B PILOT					
ATTAIN AND MAINTAIN CORE/MISSION SKILL PROFICIENCY MATRIX BY POI					
ATTAIN PROFICIENCY				MAINTAIN PROFICIENCY	
BASIC POI		REFRESHER POI			
STAGE	CODE	STAGE	CODE	STAGE	CODE
CORE SKILL (2000 Phase)					
RECSIM	S2100R	RECSIM	S2100R	RECSIM	S2100R
	S2101R		S2101R		S2101R
	S2102R		S2102R		S2102R
T2PREV	2200R	T2PREV	2200R	T2PREV	2200R
NAV	2300R	NAV	2300R	NAV	
	2301R		2301R		2301R
TACREV	2400R	TACREV	2400R	TACREV	2400R
MISSION SKILL (3000 Phase)					
OSA	3100R	OSA	3100R	OSA	3100R
ALS	3200R	ALS	3100R	ALS	3200R
S prefix and blue font = flown in simulator					
R suffix and Grey highlight = R-coded "Refresher" event					

2.5   CERTIFICATION, QUALIFICATION AND DESIGNATION TABLES. The tables
below delineate T&R events required to be completed to attain proficiency,
initial qualifications and designations. In addition to event requirements,
all required stage lectures, briefs, squadron training, prerequisites, and
other criteria shall be completed prior to completing final events.
Certification, qualification and designation letters signed by the Commanding
Officer shall be placed in Aircrew Performance Records (APR) and NATOPS
jackets. Loss of proficiency in all qualification events causes the
associated qualification to be lost. Regaining a qualification requires
completing all R-coded syllabus events associated with that qualification.

2.5.1   INSTRUCTOR DESIGNATIONS

VMR-1 C-9B PILOT INSTRUCTOR DESIGNATIONS (5000 Phase)	
INSTRUCTOR DESIGNATION	EVENTS
ANI	6500,5101 (1000 hours fixed wing time)
NI	6500,5101 (1000 hours fixed wing time)
NE	6500,5101 (1000 hours fixed wing time)

2.5.2   REQUIREMENTS, CERTIFICATIONS, QUALIFICATIONS, AND DESIGNATIONS

2.5.2.1 The tables below delineate T&R events required to be completed to
attain initial qualifications and designations. All stage lectures, briefs,
squadron training, prerequisites, and open and closed book NATOPS exams shall
be complete and graded prior to completing evaluation flights. Qualification

and designation letters signed by the Commanding Officer shall be placed in individual NATOPS and APR jackets.

VMR-1 C-9B PILOT REQUIREMENTS, CERTIFICATIONS, QUALIFICATIONS, AND DESIGNATIONS (R,C,Q,& D) [6000 Phase]	
R,C,Q,& D	EVENTS
QUALIFICATIONS	
NATOPS	6000,6001,6002,6100
STANDARD INSTRUMENT	6003,6004,6200
SPECIAL INSTRUMENT	6003,6004,6201
CRM	6005,6101
DESIGNATIONS	
T3P	6100,6300 (20 hours in C-9B)
T2P	6100,6400 (100 hours in C-9B)
TAC	6100,6500 (500 hours in C-9B)

2.6   VMR-1 C-9B PILOT PROGRAMS OF INSTRUCTION (POI). These tables reflect average time-to-train versus the minimum to maximum time-to-train parameters in the Training Progression Model.

2.6.1   A Transition C-9B Pilot shall be defined as a Marine Corps aviator who served previously as a rotary-wing aviator in the operating forces and subsequently progressed through at least T3P training. A Conversion C-9B Pilot shall be defined as a Marine Corps aviator who served previously as a fixed-wing aviator in the operating forces and subsequently progressed through at least T3P training. Differentiation between Transition and Conversion Pilots is identified here only in order to reiterate current Headquarters Marine Corps policy regarding incurred obligation following completion of C-9B flight training. The POI for Transition and Conversion C-9B Pilots is identical. Transition and Conversion pilots shall be assigned to the Basic POI.

2.6.2   An Initial C-9B Transport Pilot Under Instruction shall not fly as a required crewmember aboard an operational mission (cargo or passenger) until complete with Core Skill Introduction Training and the DESG-6300 flight. A T3P shall fly only in the right seat on an operational mission and shall not manipulate the flight controls aboard an operational mission until complete with Transport Second Pilot training and the DESG 6400 flight. However, a T3P may fly in the left seat and manipulate the flight controls aboard empty legs (no passengers and no cargo). A T2P may fly in either seat and manipulate the flight controls aboard an operational mission. The T2P qualification is established in order for the T2P to build time and experience while being given the opportunity to develop and display the headwork, situational awareness, airmanship, and flight leadership required for assignment to Transport Aircraft Commander Designation-TAC training.

2.6.3   An overseas mission requires a TAC and T2P. A T3P may serve aboard an overseas mission in addition to the required T2P.

2.6.4   Basic POI

VMR-1 C-9B PILOT BASIC POI		
Weeks	Phase of Instruction	Unit
8	Core Skill Introduction (1000 Phase)	VMR-1
1	Core Skill (2000 Phase)	VMR-1
2	Mission Skill (3000 Phase)	VMR-1

2.6.5   Refresher POI. A C-9B Pilot is required to complete Refresher C-9B Pilot training after having not flown the C-9B for over 180 days. A C-9B Pilot must have flown in the capacity as a C-9B pilot during the previous 24 months in order to be eligible for this Refresher POI. Outside of 24 months, the C-9B pilot must complete the entire syllabus. However, the requirement to begin at the T3P Syllabus for a previously-designated TAC who hasn't flown the C-9B in over 24 months may be waived by the squadron Commanding Officer. This provision allows for a previously proficient TAC, who is returning from another Duty Involving Flying - Operational (DIFOP) tour, to begin at the T2P syllabus. Refresher C-9B Pilots shall refresh at the level of the previously held designation. The only refresher flight events required are the "R" coded events for the level of refresher designation (i.e. T3P, T2P, TAC, IP, FCP). Commencement of a refresher POI is dependent upon a recommendation by the squadron Standardization Board and approval by the Commanding Officer. All decisions as to POI eligibility rest with the Commanding Officer.

2.6.6   If a C-9B pilot's annual Instrument Qualification has expired, the annual Instrument Ground School (to include the Instrument Exam) and annual Instrument Check Flight shall both be completed prior to completing the final "R" coded event for the refresher designation. For those initial C-9B PUIs who have been in a Duty Involving Flying - Denied (DIFDEN) tour for an extended period (i.e. 36 months or more), the instrument check flight shall be completed prior to the T3P Check Flight. In this case, the instrument flight proficiency requirements should be adjusted appropriately in order to account for the fact that the PUI is just beginning to develop C-9B proficiency. The annual instrument check flight standards required of a T2P for example would easily overwhelm a T3P who is just beginning to build C-9B proficiency.

VMR-1 C-9B PILOT REFRESHER POI		
Weeks	Phase of Instruction	Unit
1	Core Skill (2000 Phase)	VMR-1
2	Mission Skill (3000 Phase)	VMR-1

2.6.7   POI FOR INSTRUCTOR PILOT UNDER TRAINING (IUT). The IUT shall have been recommended by the squadron Standardization Board and approved by the squadron Commanding Officer prior to commencing this POI. All decisions as to POI eligibility rest with the Commanding Officer.

VMR-1 C-9B PILOT INSTRUCTOR POI		
Weeks	Phase of Instruction	Unit
1	Instructor Pilot Training (5000 Phase)	VMR-1

2.6.8   POI FOR FUNCTIONAL CHECK PILOT UNDER INSTRUCTION. The Functional Check Pilot Under Instruction shall have been recommended by the squadron Standardization Board and approved by the Commanding Officer prior to commencing this POI. All decisions as to POI eligibility rest with the Commanding Officer.

VMR-1 C-9B PILOT FUNCTIONAL CHECK PILOT POI		
Weeks	Phase of Instruction	Unit
1	Functional Check Flight Training (6000 Phase)	VMR-1

2.7 SYLLABUS NOTES

2.7.1 Environmental Conditions Matrix

Environmental Conditions	
Code	Meaning
D	Shall be flown during hours of daylight: (by exception - there is no use of a symbol)
N*	Shall be flown during hours of darkness must be flown unaided
(N*)	May be flown during hours of darkness - If flown during hours of darkness must be flown unaided
Note - If the event is to be flown in the simulator the Simulator Instructor shall set the desired environmental conditions for the event.	

2.7.2 Device Matrix

DEVICE (Aviation Flying)	
Symbol	Meaning
A	Flown in aircraft
A/S	Aircraft preferred may be flown in simulator
S	Flown in simulator
S/A	Simulator preferred may be flown in aircraft
Note - If the event is to be flown in the simulator the Simulator Instructor shall set the desired environmental conditions for the event.	

2.7.3 Program of Instruction Matrix

PROGRAM OF INSTRUCTION MATRIX			
Program of Instruction (POI)	Symbol	Aviation Flying	Aviation Ground
Basic	B	Initial MOS/Skill Training	Initial MOS training
Refresher	R	DIFDEN to DIFOP in same T/M/S	Return to community from non (MOS/Skill) associated tour
Maintain	M	All individuals who have attained CSP/MSP/CPP by initial POI assignment are re-assigned to the M POI to maintain proficiency.	

2.7.4 Event Terms

EVENT TERMS	
TERM	DESCRIPTION
Discuss	An explanation of systems, procedures, or maneuvers during the brief, in flight, or post flight. PUI is responsible for knowledge of procedures.
Demonstrate	The description and performance of a particular maneuver/event by the instructor, observed by the PUI. The PUI is responsible for knowledge of the procedures prior to the demonstration of a required maneuver.
Introduce	The instructor may demonstrate a procedure or maneuver to PUI, or may coach the PUI through the maneuver without demonstration. The PUI performs the procedures or maneuver with coaching as necessary. The PUI is responsible for knowledge of the procedures.
Practice	The performance of a maneuver or procedure by the PUI that may have been previously introduced in order to attain a specified level of performance.
Review	Demonstrated proficiency of a maneuver by the PUI.
Evaluate	Any flight designed to evaluate aircrew standardization that does not fit another category such as SARCK, HACCK, T2PCK, etc.
E-Coded	This term means that documentation (ATF) is required each time the event is logged. Requires evaluation by a certified standardization instructor (NATOPS I, WTI, INST Evaluator etc.)

2.7.5   Requirements For T3P Designation. 1000 Phase complete, 20 hours in the C-9B (10 of which may come from the C-9B simulator), NATOPS open and closed book tests complete, Course Rules Exam and VMR-1 SOP Exam complete, current instrument rating.

2.7.6   <u>Requirements For T2P Designation</u>. T3P designation, 100 hours in the C-9B, 800 hours total time, NATOPS open and closed book tests complete, current instrument rating.

2.7.7   <u>Requirements For TAC Designation</u>. T2P designation, 500 hours in the C-9B (20 of which may be simulator time), 1500 hours total time, NATOPS open and closed book tests complete, current instrument rating.

2.8   <u>CORE SKILL INTRODUCTION FRS ACADEMIC PHASE (0000 Phase)</u>. The squadron training events listed below will be completed prior to commencing FAM-1300 for a basic and refresher PUI.

T&R CODE	ACADEMIC SYLLABUS
	FRS ACADEMIC PHASE (0000)
ACAD-0001	Local course rules review and exam
ACAD-0002	VMR-1 C-9B SOP review and exam
ACAD-0004	Start/taxi/shutdown procedures
ACAD-0005	Post-flight inspection

2.9   <u>CORE SKILL INTRODUCTION PHASE (1000)</u>. The Core Skill Introduction Phase is designed to familiarize the PUI with C-9B normal cockpit procedures, CRM, systems operation and limitations, emergency procedures and to introduce instrument flight procedures.

2.10   <u>CORE SKILL INTRODUCTION STAGES (1000)</u>

PARAGRAPH	STAGE
2.10.1	Simulation flights (SIM)
2.10.2	Familiarization (FAM)
2.10.3	T3P Review (T3PREV)

2.10.1   <u>Simulation Flights (Initial) (SIM)</u>

2.10.1.1 <u>Purpose</u>. Provide initial simulator training in the C-9B to prepare the PUI for flight training.

2.10.1.2 <u>General</u>. Following initial simulator training, a T3P should attend refresher simulator training six months after commencing the T3P squadron flight syllabus. This prepares the T3P for evaluation and designation as a T2P. However, the six-month refresher simulator syllabus is not a prerequisite for designation as a T2P. After completion of the six-month refresher simulator syllabus, pilots should attend refresher simulator training every 12 months (not to exceed 18 months). If a C-9B Pilot goes over 18 months without simulator refresh, he will be considered down until refreshed.

2.10.1.3 <u>Crew Requirements</u>. SIM IP, PUI (Per current contract)

2.10.1.4 <u>Academic Training</u>. Prior to commencing the simulator phase of training the PUI will complete five days of ground school, consisting of items such as aircraft, systems, performance, and emergency procedures needed to complete the Simulator phase and ultimately fly the aircraft.

SIM-1100   4.0   *   B   (N*)   S(No Motion)   1 C-9B

  Goal. Per current contract.
  Requirement. Per current contract.
  Performance Standard. Per current contract.
  Prerequisite. Ground school complete.

SIM-1101   4.0   *   B   (N*)   S(No Motion)   1 C-9B

  Goal. Per current contract.
  Requirement. Per current contract.
  Performance Standard. Per current contract.
  Prerequisite. SIM-1100

SIM-1102   4.0   *   B   (N*)   S(No Motion)   1 C-9B

  Goal. Per current contract.
  Requirement. Per current contract.
  Performance Standard. Per current contract.
  Prerequisite. SIM-1101

SIM-1103   4.0   *   B   (N*)   S(No Motion)   1 C-9B

  Goal. Per current contract.
  Requirement. Per current contract.
  Performance Standard. Per current contract.
  Prerequisite. SIM-1102

SIM-1104   4.0   *   B   (N*)   S   1 C-9B

  Goal. Per current contract.
  Requirement. Per current contract.
  Performance Standard. Per current contract.
  Prerequisite. SIM-1103

SIM-1105   4.0   *   B   (N*)   S   1 C-9B

  Goal. Per current contract.
  Requirement. Per current contract.
  Performance Standard. Per current contract.
  Prerequisite. SIM-1104

SIM-1106   4.0   *   B   (N*)   S   1 C-9B

  Goal. Per current contract.
  Requirement. Per current contract.
  Performance Standard. Per current contract.
  Prerequisite. SIM-1105

SIM-1107   4.0   *   B   (N*)   S   1 C-9B

  Goal. Per current contract.
  Requirement. Per current contract.
  Performance Standard. Per current contract.
  Prerequisite. SIM-1106

SIM-1108   4.0   *   B   (N*)   S   1 C-9B

> Goal. Per current contract.
> Requirement. Per current contract.
> Performance Standard. Per current contract.
> Prerequisite. SIM-1107

SIM-1109   4.0   *   B   (N*)   S   1 C-9B

> Goal. Per current contract.
> Requirement. Per current contract.
> Performance Standard. Per current contract.
> Prerequisite. SIM-1108

SIM-1110   4.0   *   B   (N*)   S   1 C-9B

> Goal. Per current contract.
> Requirement. Per current contract.
> Performance Standard. Per current contract.
> Prerequisite. SIM-1109

SIM-1111   4.0   *   B   (N*)   S   1 C-9B

> Goal. Per current contract.
> Requirement. Per current contract.
> Performance Standard. Per current contract.
> Prerequisite. SIM-1110

2.10.2 Familiarization Flights (FAM)

2.10.2.1 Purpose. Instruct PUI in aircraft ground handling, VFR and IFR flight characteristics and limitations with emphasis on instrument flight procedures and proper response to aircraft emergency situations.

2.10.2.2 General. Pilots Under Instruction shall be in the left seat for all training flights unless otherwise noted in the training syllabus. All training flights shall be flown with a designated NATOPS Instructor with the exception of Instrument Evaluation Flights (INST-6200, INST-6201) which may be flown with any TAC who is designated on the squadron Instrument Board.

2.10.2.3 Crew Requirements. IP, PUI, CC (CC position may be filled by TAC, T2P, or T3P).

FAM-1300   3.0   *   B   D   A(Static)   1 C-9B

> Goal. Introduction to the C-9B preflight planning, checklists, preflight walk-around, emergency egress, and weight and balance.
> Requirement
>> Discuss
>>> Preflight inspection
>>> Cockpit checkout
>>> Checklists
>>> Emergency egress drill
>>> Flight planning
>>> Weight and balance
>>> Post flight inspection

Introduce

Preflight inspection
Cockpit checkout
Checklists
Emergency egress drill
Flight planning
Weight and balance
Post flight inspection

Performance Standard. Per Squadron Flight Training Instruction.

Prerequisite. SIM-1111

FAM-1301   3.0   *   B   D   A   1 C-9B

Goal. Introduce C-9B normal flight maneuvers.

Requirement

Discuss

APU
Checklists
Flight director
Departure and approach instrument set-up procedures
Engine start
Takeoff procedures
Climb
Airwork (climbs, level offs, descents, level turns,
roll rate demonstration, power management, speed changes
with/without speedbrakes, high sink rate demo, steep turns)
Approach and landing configuration (Speeds and procedures)
TOLD cards
CRM

Introduce

Engine start
Taxi
Braking and steering techniques
Crew briefing items
Static takeoff (15° flaps)
Climbs
Level offs
Descents
Level turns
Steep turns
Roll rate demonstration
Speed brake usage
High sink rate demonstration
Power management
IP demonstrated visual recovery and touch-and-go landing followed
by PUI performing touch-and-go landings and full stop landing
with auto spoiler

Review

Preflight inspection
Operation of cabin doors
Cockpit emergency equipment and exits
Cockpit checklist

Performance Standard. Per Squadron Flight Training Instruction.

Prerequisite. FAM-1300

FAM-1302   3.0   *   B   D   A   1 C-9B

    Goal. Introduce C-9B normal flight maneuvers.

    Requirement

        Discuss

            Engines/oil system
            Air conditioning system
            Radar
            INS
            FMS
            Approach/landing configuration/speeds
            Holding and procedure turns
            Missed approach
            Critical action emergency procedures
            Performance data

        Introduce
            Rolling takeoff (15° or 5° flaps)
            SFD turns
            Approach to stall series (not required if completed in simulator within last 12 months)
            Holding
             ILS/GCA
            Non-precision approaches
            Circling
            Missed approach procedures

        Review
            Preflight inspection
            Cockpit checklist
            Engine start
            Taxi
            Braking and steering techniques crew briefing items
            Steep turns
            Visual approaches to touch-and-go landings
            Full stop landings with auto spoiler

    Performance Standard. Per Squadron Flight Training Instruction.

    Prerequisite. FAM-1301

FAM-1303   3.0   *   B   D   A   1 C-9B

    Goal. Introduce emergency procedures.

    Requirement

        Discuss
            Fuel system
            Pneumatic system
            Anti-ice system
            Oxygen system
            Aborted takeoff
            Rapid decompression/emergency descent
            High altitude/high speed characteristics
            Critical action emergency procedures
            Performance data
            Simulated engine failure at V_1

        Introduce
            Start (cross bleed)
            Simulated engine failure after V_1

Use of autopilot and emergency descent
Perform visual, GCA and ILS approaches with raw data inputs,
coupled autopilot, one engine, zero flaps or slats retracted as
appropriate to touch-and-go or full stop landing
Single engine go-around and manual spoiler full-stop landing
Review
Preflight inspection
Taxi items on FAM-1300 and FAM-1301
Rolling Takeoff (15° flaps)

Performance Standard. Per Squadron Flight Training Instruction.

Prerequisite. FAM-1302

FAM-1304   3.0   *   B   N*   A   1 C-9B

Goal. Review FAM/INST maneuvers at night.

Requirement
Discuss
Electrical system
Electrical fire and smoke/fume elimination
Standard voice calls
Minimum maneuver speeds
CRM Mission Analysis and Situational Awareness
Review
Review preflight/start/taxi items covered on FAM-1300 through
FAM-1302
Perform rolling takeoff with 15° flaps
ILS and GCA approaches
Touch-and-go landings
Full stop manual spoiler landing

Performance Standard. Per Squadron Flight Training Instruction.

Prerequisite. FAM-1303

FAM-1305   3.0   *   B   D   A   1 C-9B

Goal. PUI in right seat to perform duties of copilot.

Requirement
Discuss
Fire procedures
Hydraulics/flight controls
Performance
De-rated thrust takeoff
Introduce
Engine battery start
Static takeoff (15° or 5°) flaps
De-rated thrust takeoff
Manual pressurization
Maximum performance full stop landing
Review
Preflight/start/taxi crew briefing items covered on previous
flights
All approaches and landings covered on previous flights

Performance Standard. Per Squadron Flight Training Instruction.

Prerequisite. FAM-1304

2.10.3 <u>T3P Review Flight (T3PREV)</u>

2.10.3.1 <u>Purpose</u>. Ensure T3P is well versed in ground responsibilities and exhibiting normal progression in flight responsibilities for time in aircraft.

2.10.3.3 <u>Crew Requirements</u>. IP, PUI, CC (CC position may be filled by TAC, T2P, or T3P)

T3PREV-1400 3.0 *   B   D   A   1 C-9B

    <u>Goal</u>. PUI in left or right seat at discretion of IP. Review all previously introduced material in preparation for T3P Check flight.

    <u>Requirement</u>

      Discuss

        OPARS flight planning
        Flight in high altitude structure
        Line mission considerations

      Introduce

        High altitude flight regime to include the following: Filing criteria, long range cruise considerations, and navigation procedures

      Review

        Review engine failure at V_1
        Emergency return
        Steep turns
        SFD turns
        Approach to stall series (not required if completed in simulator within last 12 months)
        Emergency descent
        Precision and non-precision approaches
        Circling approach
        Holding
        Single engine ILS
        SFD ILS
        No-flap/no-slat approach and landing
        Single engine go-around
        Manual spoiler full stop landing
        Emphasize emergency procedures and abnormal situation responses

    <u>Performance Standard</u>. Per Squadron Flight Training Instruction.

    <u>Prerequisite</u>. FAM-1305

2.11 <u>CORE SKILL PHASE (2000)</u>

2.11.1 <u>General</u>. Core Skill Phase in the C-9B provides the PUI with the necessary review flights to prepare for advancement to T2P and TAC.

2.12 <u>CORE SKILL INTRODUCTION STAGES (2000)</u>

PARAGRAPH	STAGE
2.12.1	Recurrent Simulators (RECSIM)
2.12.2	T2P Review (T2PREV)
2.12.3	Navigation (NAV)
2.12.4	TAC Review (TACREV)

2.12.1 RECURRENT SIMULATOR TRAINING (RECSIM)

2.12.1.1 Purpose. Review C-9B normal cockpit procedures, CRM, systems operation and limitations, emergency procedures, and instrument flight procedures and maintain currency.

2.12.1.2 General. Following initial simulator training, a T3P should attend Recurrent Simulator Training six months after commencing the T3P squadron flight syllabus. This prepares the T3P for evaluation and designation as a T2P. However, the six-month recurrent simulator syllabus is not a prerequisite for designation as a T2P.

2.12.1.2.1 After completion of the six-month recurrent simulator syllabus, pilots should attend recurrent simulator training every 12 months (not to exceed 18 months). If a C-9B pilot goes over 18 months without recurrent training, he will be considered down until refreshed.

2.12.1.3 Crew Requirements. SIM IP, PUI (Per current contract)

RECSIM-2100 4.0   365   B,R,M   (N*)   S   1 C-9B

>   Goal. Per current contract.
>   Requirement. Per current contract.
>   Performance Standard. Per current contract.
>   Prerequisite. SIM-1111

RECSIM-2101 4.0   365   B,R,M   (N*)   S   1 C-9B

>   Goal. Per current contract.
>   Requirement. Per current contract.
>   Performance Standard. Per current contract.
>   Prerequisite. REFSIM-2100

RECSIM-2102 4.0   365   B,R,M   (N*)   S   1 C-9B

>   Goal. Per current contract.
>   Requirement. Per current contract.
>   Performance Standard. Per current contract.
>   Prerequisite. REFSIM-2101

2.12.2 T2P Review (T2PREV)

2.12.2.1 Purpose. To prepare the PUI for the T2P check-ride.

2.12.2.2 General. Prior to flying T2PREV-2100 a PUI must have at least 100 hours in the C-9B and 800 hours total time. The time obtained during the T2PREV may be counted towards the time requirements. After completion of all T3P events flight time in the C-9B will be obtained through actual mission flights.

2.12.2.2.1 T3P will occupy the left seat to perform duties of the flying pilot.

2.12.2.3 Crew Requirements. T2PREV CREW - IP, PUI, CC (CC position may be filled by TAC, T2P, or T3P). NAV-2300, NAV-2301 CREW - Full mission crew.

T2PREV-2200 3.0   1095 B,R,M   D   A   1 C-9B

> Goal. Refine copilot performance and review all copilot duties and responsibilities.
>
> Requirement
>
>> Discuss
>>
>>> Systems and limitations
>>> Bold face emergency procedures
>>> Aircraft performance
>>
>> Review
>>
>>> Review preflight/start/taxi crew briefing
>>> FMS/GPS/INS operation
>>> Engine failure at V_1
>>> Emergency return
>>> Steep turns
>>> SFD turns
>>> Approach to stall series (not required if completed in simulator within last 12 months)
>>> Emergency descent
>>> Precision and non-precision approaches
>>> Circling approach
>>> Holding
>>> Single engine ILS
>>> Single engine go around
>>> SFD ILS
>>> No-flap/no-slat approach and landing
>>> Manual spoiler full-stop landing
>>> Emphasize emergency procedures and abnormal situation responses
>
> Performance Standard. Per Squadron Flight Training Instruction.
>
> Prerequisite. DESG-6200, 100 hrs in C-9B, 800 total hrs

2.12.3   Navigational Route Checks (NAV)

2.12.3.1 Purpose. Conduct both an overland and overwater route check flight prior to upgrade to TAC.

2.12.3.2 General. The TAC Route Check (NAV-2300) should be conducted on an operational mission with a full crew. The TAC Overwater Check (NAV-2301) may be conducted with either minimum crew on a dedicated training mission or on an operational mission with a full crew.

2.12.3.2.1 The overwater check flight for T2P prior to upgrade to TAC can also be logged to maintain ICAO proficiency for the TAC (6 month refly *). Flight must include a Remain Overnight (RON) and an overwater leg of at least 1,300 nautical miles.

NAV-2300   5.0   *   B,R   (N*) E   A   1 C-9B

> Goal. PUI performs extended range operations and alternates between left and right seats throughout the mission in order to demonstrate flight leadership from either seat. T2P shall also demonstrate the ability to supervise preflight preparation and manage a crew and aircraft away from home station on an operational mission that includes a Remain Overnight (RON).
>
> Requirement

Discuss

Mission coordination
Flight planning
Weather
Fuel planning
Load computations
Performance
CRM

Review

PUI shall demonstrate flight leadership and crew resource
management by acting as the TAC during an operational mission
that includes an RON. During the trip, the T2P shall conduct a
two-engine instrument approach and landing from the right seat.

Performance Standard. Per Squadron Flight Training Instruction.

Prerequisite. DESG-6300

NAV-2301   5.0   180   B,R,M   (N*)   E   A   1 C-9B

Goal. PUI conducts overwater navigation. Evaluation legs should be
conducted with the PUI in the right seat. TAC/T2P to demonstrate the
ability to manage a crew and aircraft on an extended, overwater flight
under ICAO rules.

Requirement

Discuss

Mission coordination
Crew briefing
ATFP briefing coordination
Confirmation Brief
Flight planning
Weather brief
Fuel planning
Weight and balance
Aircraft inspection
Cargo inspection (as required)
Manifest inspection
Flight advisory message review
Aircraft and Personnel Automated Clearance System (APACS) review
Foreign clearance guide review
Navigation pubs pack up
Survival gear inspection
Fuel computations
Performance
Supervise loadmaster in arranging for billeting
Crew ground transportation
Customs and agriculture inspection

Review

TAC/T2P to conduct overwater navigation in accordance with ICAO
convention, from the right seat. During the trip, the TAC/T2P
shall conduct a two-engine instrument approach and landing from
the right seat.

Performance Standard. Per Squadron Flight Training Instruction.

Prerequisite. DESG-6300

2.12.4   TAC Review (TACREV)

2.12.4.1 Purpose. Review all previously covered items and ensure that the T2P is adequately prepared for a TAC check.

2.12.4.2 Crew Requirements. IP, PUI, CC (CC position may be filled by TAC, T2P, or T3P)

TACREV-2400 3.0   1095   B,R,M   (N*)   A   1 C-9B

> Goal. Review all C-9B previous NATOPS normal and emergency procedures. Demonstrate ability to lead and coordinate crew during emergencies, plus meet all previous NATOPS requirements.
>
> Requirement. T2P will fly from left seat.

>> Discuss
>>> Similar to the brief required for DESG-6300 except that the PUI shall demonstrate a more extensive, in-depth knowledge of systems and limitations, bold-face emergency procedures, warning and caution lights, bold-face immediate action procedures, and performance. Additionally, the PUI shall demonstrate a working knowledge of all governing operational directives such as NATOPS, OPNAV 3710, FAR/AIM, ICAO convention, SOP, and FTI.

>> Review
>>> Aircraft data book (ADB)
>>> Engine failure at V_1
>>> Emergency return
>>> Steep turns
>>> Clean approach to stall
>>> SFD turns
>>> Approach to stall series (not required if completed in simulator within last 12 months)
>>> Emergency descent
>>> Precision and non-precision approaches
>>> Circling approach
>>> Holding
>>> Single engine ILS
>>> Single engine go around
>>> SFD ILS
>>> No-flap/no-slat approach and landing
>>> Manual spoiler full-stop landing
>>> Emphasize emergency procedures and abnormal situation responses
>>> Event shall conclude with a review of M-SHARP flight data entry

> Performance Standard. Per Squadron Flight Training Instruction.
>
> Prerequisite. NAV-2300, NAV-2301

2.13   MISSION SKILLS PHASE (3000)

2.13.1   General. The Mission Skill Phase is designed to familiarize the PUI with the unique missions and challenges associated with the VMR-1, C-9B. Mission Skills are designed to fulfill the requirements of the C-9B Mission Essential Task List as defined by the associated Marine Corps Task (MCT).

2.14   MISSION SKILL STAGES (3000)

PARAGRAPH	STAGE
2.14.1	Operational Support Airlift (OSA)
2.14.2	Air Logistical Support (ALS)

2.14.1 Operational Support Airlift (OSA)

2.14.1.1 Purpose. This event is designed to fulfill the requirement set in MCT 1.3.4.1.2, conduct OSA.

2.14.1.2 General. It is understood that many missions will be a combination of both passenger and cargo transportation and both codes will be used when filling out the NAVFLIR. Both codes are made available for flights that clearly fall into a single category.

*Note: A TAC should not fly as the signing TAC aboard an overwater mission if it has been over 6 months since returning from the last overwater mission. This requirement may be waived up to 12 months at the discretion of the Squadron Commanding Officer in order to account for a TAC who has a considerable amount of previous C-9B overseas experience.

2.14.1.3 Crew Requirement. Full mission crew.

OSA-3100   3.0   180   B,R,M   (N*)   A   1   C-9B

   Goal. Introduce the T3P to the JOSAC passenger mission or provide continued update to the skills of the T2P and TAC while performing the mission in their different aircrew roles.

   Requirement. Aircrew will execute a JOSAC passenger mission and perform all pilot flight related duties safely and proficiently.

   Performance Standard. Per JOSAC/ASM tasking, NATOPS, SOP, and FAA or ICAO standards and regulations.

   Prerequisite. DESG-6200

2.14.2   Air Logistics Support (ALS)

2.14.2.1 Purpose. This event is designed to fulfill the requirement set in MMC 4.3.8, Conduct Air Logistics Support.

2.14.2.2 General. It is understood that many missions will be a combination of both passenger and cargo transportation and both codes will be used when filling out the NAVFLIR. Both codes are made available for flights that clearly fall into a single category.

2.14.2.3 Crew Requirement. Full mission crew.

ALS-3200   3.0   180   B,R,M   (N*)   A   1   C-9B

   Goal. Introduce the T3P to the C-9B cargo mission or provide continued update to the skills of the T2P and TAC while performing the mission in their different aircrew roles.

   Requirement. Aircrew will execute a JOSAC cargo mission and perform all pilot flight related duties safely and proficiently.

   Performance Standard. Per JOSAC/ASM tasking, NATOPS, SOP, and FAA or ICAO standards and regulations.

   Prerequisite. DESG-6200

2.15   CORE PLUS SKILL PHASE (4000)

2.15.1   General. There is no Core Plus Skill Phase in the C-9B T&R.

2.16   CORE PLUS SKILL STAGES (4000)

2.16.1   General. There are no 4000 level events in the C-9B T&R.

2.17   INSTRUCTOR TRAINING PHASE (5000)

2.17.1   General. The instructor training phase is designed to provide the Squadron with a cadre of qualified instructors needed to ensure quality training at all times.

2.18   INSTRUCTOR TRAINING STAGES

PARAGRAPH	STAGE
2.18.1	Instructor Under Training (IUT)

2.18.1   Instructor Under Training (IUT)

2.18.1.1 Purpose. Develop qualified instructor pilots with the ability to teach all phases of C-9B flight and mission requirements.

2.18.1.2 General. An IP is qualified to instruct in all phases of aircraft operations. SqdnO P3710.1 series (VMR-1 SOP for Flight Operations) delineates duties that may be performed.

2.18.1.2 Crew Requirements. IP, PUI, CC (CC position may be filled by TAC, T2P, or T3P)

IUT-5100   3.0   *   B   (N*)   E   A   1 C-9B

    Goal. Instruction introduction. IUT in right seat.
    Requirement
        Brief/Discuss
            Exchange of flight controls
            Conduct of training flight
            Instructional techniques
        Review
            IUT will coach IP on taxi procedures
            IUT conducts:
            Normal takeoff and initiates a simulated engine failure post V_1
            and demonstrates an emergency return
            Steep turns
            High-sink rate recovery
            Approach to stall series (not required if completed in simulator
             within last 12 months)

            Emergency descent
            Holding
            Precision and non-precision approaches
            Single engine approach
            Single engine go-around
            No-flap/no slat approach and landing
            Circling
            Manual spoiler full stop landing

Exchange of flight controls at a safe taxi speed
Demonstrate ability to perform all maneuvers in standardized
manner and to recognize and correct common student errors

Performance Standard. Pilot shall demonstrate the ability to instruct
familiarization and instrument maneuvers, including demonstrating and
introducing maneuvers to pilots under instruction.

Prerequisite. DESG-6400

IUT-5101   3.0   *   B,R   (N*)   E   A   1 C-9B

Goal. IUT evaluation flight. IUT in right seat.

Requirement.

Discuss

Exchange of flight controls
Conduct of evaluation flight

Review

IUT in right seat coaches IP through taxi procedures.
IUT conducts:
Normal takeoff and initiates a simulated engine failure post V_1
and demonstrates an emergency return
Steep turns
High-sink rate recovery
Approach to stall series (not required if completed in simulator
within last 12 months) Emergency descent
Holding
Precision and non-precision approaches
Single engine approach
Single engine go-around
No-flap/no slat approach and landing
Circling
Manual spoiler full stop landing
Exchange of flight controls at a safe taxi speed
Demonstrate ability to perform all maneuvers in standardized
manner, and to recognize and correct common student errors.

Performance Standard. IUT shall demonstrate the requisite maturity,
airmanship, instructional ability, and standardization expected of an
Instructor pilot.

Prerequisite. IUT-5100

2.19   REQUIREMENTS, CERTIFICATIONS, QUALIFICATIONS, AND DESIGNATIONS
(RCQD) PHASE (6000)

2.19.1   General. The 6000 phase encompasses the events required to maintain
currency with all certifications, qualifications, and designations.

2.20   REQUIREMENTS, CERTIFICATIONS, QUALIFICATIONS, AND DESIGNATIONS
(RCQD) STAGES (6000)

PARAGRAPH	STAGE
2.20.1	Academics (ACAD)
2.20.2	NATOPS (NTPS)
2.20.3	Instruments (INST)
2.20.4	Designations (DESG)
2.20.5	Functional Check Flight (FCF)

2.20.1   Academics (ACAD)

2.20.1.1 Purpose. To complete the academic requirements for subsequent
annual evaluation flights.

ACAD-6000   4.0   365   B,R,M   E

Goal. The open book examination shall consist of, but not limited to,
the question bank. The purpose of the open book examination is to
evaluate the pilot's knowledge of the appropriate publications and the
aircraft.

Performance Standard. Achieve a minimum score of 3.5 on the open book
examination.

ACAD-6001   1.5   365   B,R,M   E

Goal. The purpose of the closed book examination is to evaluate the
pilot's knowledge of the concerning normal/emergency procedures and
aircraft limitations.

Performance Standard. Achieve a minimum score of 3.3 on the closed
book examination.

Prerequisite. ACAD-6000

ACAD-6002   2.0   365   B,R,M   E

Goal. The oral examination shall consist of, but not be limited to the
question bank. The instructor may draw upon their experience to
propose questions of a direct and positive manner and in no way be
opinionated to evaluate the pilot's knowledge of the concerning
normal/emergency procedures, aircraft limitations, and performance.

Performance Standard. Achieve a minimum grade of qualified on the oral
examination.

Prerequisite. NTPS-6000 and NTPS-6001 within 60 days preceding this
event.

ACAD-6003   8.0   365   B,R,M   E

Goal. The Instrument Ground School shall be an approved Commander
Naval Air Forces (CNAF) approved syllabus.

Performance Standard.   Successfully complete Instrument Ground School.

ACAD-6004   2.0   365   B,R,M   E

Goal. Complete the instrument exam.

Performance Standard. Achieve a minimum grade of qualified on the NATOPS instrument examination.

Prerequisite. ACAD-6003

ACAD-6005   2.0   365   B,R,M   E

Goal. CRM ground instruction in accordance with applicable directives and instructions.

Performance Standard. Demonstrate satisfactory knowledge of CRM principles and their application.

ACAD-6006   1.0   30   B,R,M   E

Goal. Monthly Emergency Procedures Exam.

Requirement. Conduct a monthly EP Exam per NAVMC 3500.14.

2.20.2   NATOPS Evaluations (NTPS)

2.20.2.1 Purpose. Provide annual NATOPS and CRM evaluation flights.

NTPS-6100   1.5   365   B,R,M   (N*)   E   S/A   1 C-9B

Goal. Conduct annual NATOPS evaluation.

Requirement. Proficiency in the utilization of all aspects of the C-9B. The proficiency expected by the evaluator in this flight shall be commensurate with the experience of the pilot under evaluation.

Performance Standard. The performance expected by the evaluator in this flight shall be commensurate with the experience level of the pilot under evaluation.

Prerequisite. 6000,6001,6002

NTPS-6101   1.5   365   B,R,M   (N*)   E   S/A   1 C-9B

Goal. Conduct annual CRM evaluation.

Requirement. Perform initial/annual CRM flight evaluation per applicable directives. May be flown in conjunction with annual NATOPS evaluation flight.

Performance Standard. Performance standards will be according to the C-9B NFM.

Prerequisite. ACAD-6005

NTPS-6102   1.0   90   B,R,M   (N)   E   S/A   1 C-9B

Goal. Emergency Procedure Review.

Requirement. This event will review C-9B emergency procedures and fulfills the requirement of quarterly EP simulator training per NAVMC 3500.14. This event can be accomplished as a combined event in the simulator or in the actual aircraft while airborne or sitting on the deck.

Performance Standard. Comply with C-9B NFM emergency procedures.

2.20.3 <u>Instrument Evaluation (INST)</u>

2.20.3.1 <u>Purpose</u>. To provide annual instrument evaluation flights.

INST-6200   3.0   365   B,R,M   (N)   E   S/A   1 C-9B

> <u>Goal</u>. Complete standard instrument flight evaluation. Following completion of the ground evaluation events, a standard instrument flight/simulator evaluation event shall be flown and completed with a grade of "Qualified." Conduct an objective evaluation of the airman's knowledge of flight planning, filing, briefing, conduct of flight under normal operating conditions, emergency procedures, closing out flight plans, and debriefing.
> <u>Requirement</u>. Successfully pass the instrument check.
>
> <u>Performance Standard</u>. Executes flight and ground operations safely IAW OPNAV 3710.7 Series, Platform NATOPS, NATOPS Instrument Flight Manual, and training rules. All areas on the instrument flight evaluation are critical. An "Unsatisfactory" grade in any area shall result in an "Unsatisfactory" grade for the flight.
> <u>Prerequisite</u>. 6003, 6004, and minimum experience per OPNAVINST 3710.7.

INST-6201   3.0   365   B,R,M   (N)   E   S/A   1 C-9B

> <u>Goal</u>. Complete special instrument flight evaluation. Following completion of the ground evaluation events, a special instrument flight/simulator evaluation event shall be flown and completed with a grade of "Qualified." Conduct an objective evaluation of the airman's knowledge of flight planning, filing, briefing, conduct of flight under normal operating conditions, emergency procedures, closing out flight plans, and debriefing.
> <u>Requirement</u>. Successfully pass the instrument check.
>
> <u>Performance Standard</u>. Executes flight and ground operations safely IAW OPNAV 3710.7 series, platform NATOPS, NATOPS Instrument Flight Manual, and training rules. All areas on the instrument flight evaluation are critical. An "Unsatisfactory" grade in any area shall result in an "Unsatisfactory" grade for the flight.
> <u>Prerequisite</u>. 6003, 6004, and posses minimum experience per OPNAVINST 3710.7.

2.20.4 <u>Designation Flights (DESG)</u>

2.20.4.1 <u>Purpose</u>. To provide T3P, T2P, and TAC designated pilots.

2.20.4.2 <u>General</u>

2.20.4.2.1 A T3P must have at least 20 hours in the C-9B (10 of which may come from the C-9B simulator) before he/she can be designated.

2.20.4.2.2 A T2P must have 100 hours in the C-9B (20 of which may come from the C-9B simulator) and 800 hours total time before he/she can be designated.

2.20.4.2.3 For TAC, the intent is to ensure that a C-9B pilot has been exposed to C-9B flight operations during all four seasons prior to designation. This generally corresponds with the point at which a C-9B pilot has obtained the 500 hours in the C-9B (20 of which may come from the C-9B simulator) required for designation as a TAC. Total flight time required before this flight may be flown is 1000 fixed wing time.

DESG-6300   3.0   *   B   (N*)   E   A   1 C-9B

   Goal. T3P evaluation flight. PUI to demonstrate the ability to meet
   NATOPS qualification per Chapter 18 NATOPS evaluation criteria. The
   flight evaluation is designed to measure with maximum objectivity the
   degree of standardization demonstrated by the PUI and to ensure safety
   of flight.

   Requirement

      Brief/Discuss

         Systems and limitations
         Bold-face emergency procedures

      Review

         Engine failure at V_1
         Emergency return
         Steep turns
         SFD turns
         Approach to stall series (not required if completed in simulator
         within last 12 months)
         Emergency descent
         Precision and non-precision approaches
         Circling approach
         Holding
         Single engine ILS
         SFD ILS
         No-flap/no-slat approach and landing
         Manual spoiler full-stop landing

   Performance Standard. The T3P Check should emphasize only those areas
   that are germane to copilot duties and demonstrated performance
   required to safely terminate a flight in the event of aircraft
   commander incapacitation.

   Prerequisite. 1000 series complete

DESG-6400   3.0   *   B,R   (N*)   E   A   1 C-9B

   Goal. T2P evaluation flight. PUI to demonstrate the ability to meet
   NATOPS qualification per Chapter 18 NATOPS evaluation criteria.

   Requirement

      Brief/Discuss

         PUI should demonstrate a thorough knowledge of:
         NATOPS systems and limitations,
         Bold-face emergency procedures
         Annunciator lights

      Review

         Engine failure at V_1
         Emergency return
         Steep turns
         SFD turns
         Approach to stall series (Not required if completed in simulator
          within last 12 months)
         Emergency descent
         Precision and non-precision approaches
         Circling approach
         Holding
         Single engine ILS

SFD ILS
No-flap/no-slat approach and landing
Manual spoiler full-stop landing

Performance Standard. The flight evaluation is designed to measure with maximum objectivity the degree of standardization demonstrated by the PUI and his/her ability to handle the aircraft under any circumstances. Primary emphasis shall be placed on emergency procedures, flying skill, command mentality, and judgment.

Prerequisite. T2PREV-2100

DESG-6500   3.0   *   B,R   (N*)   E   A   1 C-9B

Goal. TAC evaluation flight. PUI to demonstrate the ability to meet NATOPS qualification per Chapter 18 NATOPS evaluation criteria. Review all C-9B previous NATOPS normal and emergency procedures. Demonstrate ability to lead and coordinate crew during emergencies, plus meet all previous NATOPS requirements. T2P in the left seat.

Requirement

Brief/Discuss. Similar to the brief required for DESG-6300 except that the T2P shall demonstrate a more extensive, in depth knowledge of:

Systems and limitations
Bold-face emergency procedures
Warning and caution lights
Performance
Additionally, the PUI shall demonstrate a working knowledge of all governing operational directives such as NATOPS, OPNAV 3710, FAR/AIM, ICAO convention, SOP, and FTI.

Review

Aircraft data book (ADB)
Engine failure at V_1
Emergency return
Steep turns
Clean approach to stall
SFD turns
Approach to stall series (not required if completed in simulator within last 12 months)
Emergency descent
Precision and non-precision approaches
Circling approach
Holding
Single engine ILS
Single engine go around
SFD ILS
No-flap/no-slat approach and landing
Manual spoiler full-stop landing
Emphasize emergency procedures and abnormal situation responses
Event shall conclude with a review of M-SHARP flight data entry

Performance Standard. The flight evaluation is designed to measure with maximum objectivity the degree of standardization demonstrated by the PUI and his/her ability to handle the aircraft under any circumstances. Primary emphasis shall be placed on emergency procedures, flying skill, command mentality, and judgment.

Prerequisite. TACREV-2300

2.20.5 Functional Check Flight (FCP)

2.20.5.1 Purpose. To qualify pilots as functional check pilots.

FCF-6600   4.0   *   B   D   E   A   1 C-9B

> Goal. Familiarize the PUI with the FCF checklist and procedures.
> Conduct training for designation as a FCP. Per a locally generated
> syllabus, conduct FCP training with a previously designated FCP.
>
> Requirement. PUI in right seat.
>
>> Brief/Discuss
>>
>>> Flight procedures/conduct
>>> FCF requirements
>>> FCF procedures
>>
>> Introduce/Practice
>>
>>> QA/maintenance brief
>>> ADB review
>>> Exterior/interior inspection
>>> Engine start
>>> Taxi
>>> Takeoff
>>> Climb
>>> Level at altitude
>>> FCF checks
>>> Enroute descent
>>> Penetration
>>> Landing
>>> Post flight
>>> Debrief QA/maintenance
>>> Sign off FCF card and required maintenance paperwork
>
> Performance Standard. PUI will demonstrate a thorough knowledge of
> aircraft performance and systems and a working knowledge of FCF
> procedures.
>
> Prerequisite. DESIG-6500

FCF-6601   4.0   *   B,R   D   E   A   1 C-9B

> Goal. Per a locally generated syllabus, conduct FCP evaluation with a
> previously designated FCP.
>
> Requirement. PUI in right seat.
>
>> Brief/Discuss
>>
>>> Flight procedures/conduct
>>> FCF requirements
>>> FCF procedures
>>
>> Introduce/Practice
>>
>>> QA/Maintenance brief
>>> ADB review
>>> Exterior/interior inspection
>>> Engine start
>>> Taxi
>>> Takeoff
>>> Climb
>>> Level at altitude
>>> FCF checks

Enroute descent
Penetration
Landing
Postflight
Debrief QA/maintenance
Sign off FCF card and required maintenance paperwork

Performance Standard. PUI will demonstrate a thorough knowledge of aircraft performance, systems, and FCF procedures.

Prerequisite. FCF-6600

2.21 AVIATION CAREER PROGRESSION MODEL (8000)

2.21.1 Purpose. To enhance professional understanding of Marine Aviation and the MAGTF, and to ensure individuals possess the requisite skills to fill battle command and battle staff positions in support of the ACE and the MAGTF in a joint environment. The focus of training in the Aviation Career Progression Model (ACPM) is on academic events in the following areas:

Marine Air Command and Control System (MACCS)

Aviation Ground Support

Joint Air Operations

ACE Battle Staff

MAGTF

Seabased Operations

Combatant Commander Organizations

2.21.1.2 All tactical T/M/S T&R manuals have ACPM training requirements embedded within the progressive training phases, including the flight leadership POI. If not already completed prior to assignment to VMR-1, pilots shall complete ACPM training requirements as outlined per their original T/M/S MOS T&R manual. Refer to NAVMC 3500.14, Aviation T&R Program Manual, as a primary reference for ACPM training requirements.

2.21.2 General. ACPM events may be conducted in group session with an assigned instructor teaching the period of instruction or they may be accomplished by self-paced instruction.

2.21.2.1 MAWTS-1 is responsible for the update and validity of the ACPM periods of instruction. In the future, courses may be consolidated or revised to meet changing requirements. Refer to the MAWTS-1 ACPM link for the current ACPM program of instruction:

https://www.intranet.tecom.usmc.mil/sites/mawts1/aviation%20career%20progression%20model/forms/allitems.aspx

2.22 T&R ATTAIN AND MAINTAIN SYLLABUS MATRICES

VMR-1 C-9B
PILOT
CORE/MISSION/CORE PLUS ATTAIN & MAINTAIN MATRIX

CORE SKILLS INTRODUCTION (1000 PHASE)

T&R DESCRIPTION	STAGE	CODE	RE FLY	BASIC POI STAGE	BASIC POI CODE	REFRESHER POI STAGE	REFRESHER POI CODE	MAINTAIN POI STAGE	MAINTAIN POI CODE	PREREQUISITES	CHAINING
Local Course Rules	ACAD	0001	*	ACAD	0001	ACAD	0001	ACAD			
SOF Review and Exam	ACAD	0002	*		0002		0002				
Start/Taxi/Shutdown	ACAD	0003	*		0003		0003				
Post-Flight Inspection	ACAD	0004	*		0004		0004				
Per current contract	SIM	1100	*	SIM	1100	SIM		SIM		0001,0002,0003,0004	
Per current contract	SIM	1101	*		1101					1100	
Per current contract	SIM	1102	*		1102					1101	
Per current contract	SIM	1103	*		1103					1102	
Per current contract	SIM	1104	*		1104					1103	
Per current contract	SIM	1105	*		1105					1104	
Per current contract	SIM	1106	*		1106					1105	
Per current contract	SIM	1107	*		1107					1106	
Per current contract	SIM	1108	*		1108					1107	
Per current contract	SIM	1109	*		1109					1108	
Per current contract	SIM	1110	*		1110					1109	
Per current contract	SIM	1111	*		1111					1110	
Preflight	FAM	1300	*	FAM	1300	FAM		FAM		0001,0002,0003,0004,1111	
Into Norm Flight Man	FAM	1301	*		1301					1300	
Rev Norm Flight Man	FAM	1302	*		1302					1301	
Intro EPs	FAM	1303	*		1303					1302	
FAM/Night Maneuvers	FAM	1304	*		1304					1303	
Right seat duties	FAM	1305	*		1305					1304	
T3P Review	T3PREV	1400	*	T3PREV	1400	T3PREV		T3PREV		1305	

CORE SKILLS PROFICIENCY (2000 PHASE)

T&R DESCRIPTION	STAGE	CODE	RE FLY	BASIC POI STAGE	BASIC POI CODE	REFRESHER POI STAGE	REFRESHER POI CODE	MAINTAIN POI STAGE	MAINTAIN POI CODE	PREREQUISITES	CHAINING
Per current contract	RECSIM	S2100	365	RECSIM	S2100R	RECSIM	S2100R	RECSIM	S2100R	1111	
Per current contract	RECSIM	S2101	365		S2101R		S2101R		S2101R	2100	
Per current contract	RECSIM	S2102	365		S2102R		S2102R		S2102R	2101	
T2P Review Flight	T2PREV	2200	1095	T2PREV	2200R	T2PREV	2200R	T2PREV	2200R	6200, 100 hrs in C-9B, 800 hrs total time	
Overland Navigation	NAV	2300	*	NAV	2300R	NAV	2300R	NAV	2300R	6300	
Overwater Navigation	NAV	2301	180		2301R		2301R	NAV	2301R	6300	
TAC Review Flight	TACREV	2400	1095	TACREV	2400R	TACREV	2400R	TACREV	2400R	2300, 2301	2200

MISSION SKILLS (3000 PHASE)

T&R EVENT INFORMATION				ATTAIN PROFICIENCY				MAINTAIN PROFICIENCY		PREREQUISITES	CHAINING
				BASIC POI		REFRESHER POI					
T&R DESCRIPTION	STAGE	CODE	RE FLY	STAGE	CODE	STAGE	CODE	STAGE	CODE		
Passenger Mission	OSA	3100	180	OSA	3100	OSA	3100R	OSA	3100R	6300	3200
Cargo Mission	ALS	3200	180	ALS	3200	ALS	3200R	ALS	3200R	6300	3100

2.23   T&R SYLLABUS MATRIX

VMRL1 PILOT T&R MATRIX

STAGE	TRNG CODE	T&R DESCRIPTION	POI	DEVICE	# OF A/C	CON	RE FLY	# OF ACAD	ACAD TIME	# OF SIM	SIM TIME	# OF FLTS	FLT TIME	PREREQUISITE	NOTES	CHAINING	EVENT CONV
		CORE SKILL INTRODUCTION TRAINING (1000 PHASE EVENTS)															
		ACADEMICS (ACAD)															
ACAD	0001	Local Course Rules	B,R				*		0.0								
ACAD	0002	SOP Review and Exam	B,R				*		0.0								
ACAD	0003	Contr w/ Taxi/Shutdown	B,R				*		0.0								
ACAD	0004	Static Flight Insp	B,R				*		0.0								
		SIMULATOR (SIM)															
SIM	1100	Per current contract	B	S		(N*)	*				4.0			0001,0002,0003,0004	No Motion		105
SIM	1101	Per current contract	B	S		(N*)	*				4.0			1100	No Motion		106
SIM	1102	Per current contract	B	S		(N*)	*				4.0			1101	No Motion		107
SIM	1103	Per current contract	B	S		(N*)	*				4.0			1102	No Motion		108
SIM	1104	Per current contract	B	S		(N*)	*				4.0			1103	No Motion		109
SIM	1105	Per current contract	B	S		(N*)	*				4.0			1104			110
SIM	1106	Per current contract	B	S		(N*)	*				4.0			1105			111
SIM	1107	Per current contract	B	S		(N*)	*				4.0			1106			112
SIM	1108	Per current contract	B	S		(N*)	*				4.0			1107			113
SIM	1109	Per current contract	B	S		(N*)	*				4.0			1108			114
SIM	1110	Per current contract	B	S		(N*)	*				4.0			1109			115
SIM	1111	Per current contract	B	S		(N*)	*				4.0			1110			116
		TOTAL SIM STAGE						0	0.0	12	48.0	0	0.0				
		FAMILIARIZATION (FAM)															

VMGR-1 PILOT T&R MATRIX

STAGE	TRNG CODE	T&R DESCRIPTION	POI (E)	DEVICE	# OF A/C	CON	RE FLY	# OF ACAD	ACAD TIME	# OF SIM	SIM TIME	# OF FLTS	FLT TIME	PREREQUISITE	NOTES	CHAINING	EVENT CONV
FAM	1300	Preflight	B	A	1	D	*						3.0	0001,0002,0003,0004,1111			130
FAM	1301	Into flight maneuvers	B	A	1	D	*						3.0	1300			131
FAM	1302	Rev flight maneuvers	B	A	1	D	*						3.0	1301			132
FAM	1303	Intro EPs	B	A	1	D	*						3.0	1302			133
FAM	1304	FAM/Night Maneuvers	B	A	1	N*	*						3.0	1303			134
FAM	1305	Right Seat duties	B	A	1	D	*						3.0	1303			140
		TOTAL FAM STAGE						0	0.0	0	0.0	6	18.0				
		T3P REVIEW (T3PREV)															
T3PREV	1400	T3P Review	B	A	1	D	*						3.0	1305			141
		TOTAL T3P STAGE						0	0.0	0	0.0	1	3.0				
		TOTAL CORE SKILL INTRODUCTION PHASE (1000 PHASE)						4	8.0	12	48.0	7	21.0				
		CORE SKILL TRAINING (2000 PHASE EVENTS)															
		RECURRENT SIMULATORS (RECSIM)															
RECSIM	2100	Per current contract	B,R,M	S		(N*)	365				4.0			1111			117
RECSIM	2101	Per current contract	B,R,M	S		(N*)	365				4.0			2100			118
RECSIM	2102	Per current contract	B,R,M	S		(N*)	365				4.0			2101			119
		TOTAL RECSIM STAGE								3	12.0						
		T2P REVIEW (T2PREV)															
T2PREV	2200	T2P Review Flight	B,R,M	A	1	D	1095						3.0	6300, 100 hrs in C-9B, 800 hrs. total time.			200
		TOTAL T2PREV STAGE						0	0.0	0	0.0	1	3.0				
		NAVIGATION (NAV)															
NAV	2300	Overland Nav	B,R	A	1	(N*)	*						5.0	6300			300
NAV	2301	Overwater Nav	B,R,M	A	1	(N*)	180						5.0	6300			310
		TOTAL NAV STAGE						0	0.0	0	0.0	2	10.0				
		TAC REVIEW (TACREV)															
TACREV	2400	TAC Review Flight	B,R,M	A	1	(N*)	1095			0	0.0	1	3.0	2000 Phase Complete		2200	320
		TOTAL TACREV STAGE						0	0.0	0	0.0	1	3.0				
		TOTAL CORE SKILL PHASE (2000 PHASE)						0	0.0	3	12.0	4	16.0				
		MISSION SKILL TRAINING (3000 PHASE)															
		OPERATIONAL SUPPORT AIRLIFT (OSA)															
OSA	3100	Passenger Mission	B,R,M	A	1	(N*)	180						3.0	6300		3200	
		TOTAL OSA STAGE						0	0.0	0	0.0	1	3.0				
		AIR LOGISTICS SUPPORT (ALS)															
ALS	3200	Cargo Mission	B,R,M	A	1	(N*)	180						3.0	6300		3100	
		TOTAL ALS STAGE						0	0.0	0	0.0	1	3.0				

Enclosure (1)

VMR-1 PILOT T&R MATRIX

STAGE	TRNG CODE	T&R DESCRIPTION	POI	DEVICE E	DEVICE	# OF A/C	CON	RE FLY	# OF ACAD	ACAD TIME	# OF SIM	SIM TIME	# OF FLT SIM	FLT TIME	PREREQUISITE	NOTES	CHAINING	EVENT CONV
		TOTAL MISSION SKILL PHASE (3000 PHASE)															
		TOTAL 1000, 2000, & 3000 PHASE							0	0.0	0	0.0	2	6.0				
									0	0.0	15	60.0	13	43.0				
		INSTRUCTOR TRAINING (5000 PHASE EVENTS)																
		INSTRUCTOR TRAINING (5000 PHASE) (IUT)																
IUT	5100	Instructor Intro	R	E	A	1	(N*)	*						3.0	6500			500
IUT	5101	Instructor Eval	B,R	E	A	1	(N*)	*						3.0	5100			501
		TOTAL IUT STAGE							0	0.0	0	0.0	2	6.0				
		INSTRUCTOR TRAINING (5000 PHASE EVENTS) TOTAL							0	0.0	0	0.0	2	6.0				
		REQUIREMENT, QUALIFICATIONS, AND DESIGNATIONS (RQD) (6000 PHASE)																
		RQD ACADEMICS (ACAD)																
ACAD	6000	NATOPS Open Exam	B,R,M	E				365		4.0								
ACAD	6001	NATOPS Closed Exam	B,R,M	E				365		1.5					6000			
ACAD	6002	NATOPS Oral Exam	B,R,M	E				365		2.0					6000,6001			
ACAD	6003	Instrument Ground School	B,R,M	E				365		8.0								
ACAD	6004	Instrument Exam	B,R,M	E				365		2.0					6003			
ACAD	6005	CRM Ground Class	B,R,M	E				365		2.0								
ACAD	6006	Monthly EP Exam	B,R,M	E				30		1.0								
		TOTAL ACAD STAGE							7	20.5	0	0.0	0	0.0				
		NATOPS																
NTPS	6100	NATOPS Evaluation	B,R,M	E	A/S	1	(N*)	365						1.5	6000,6001,6002		2400,2200	500
NTPS	6101	CRM Flight Evaluation	B,R,M	E	A/S	1	(N*)	365						1.5	6005			
NTPS	6102	Emergency Procedures Review	B,R,M	E	A/S	1	(N*)	90						1.0				
		NATOPS TOTAL							0	0.0	0	0.0	3	4.0				
		INSTRUMENT (INST)																
INST	6200	Stan Instrument Eval	B,R,M	E	S/A	1	(N*)	365				3.0		0.0	6003,6004		6101	601
INST	6201	Spec Instrument Eval	B,R,M	E	S/A	1	(N*)	365				3.0		0.0	6003,6004		6101,6200	
		TOTAL INST STAGE							0	0.0	2	6.0	0	0.0				
		T3P, T2P, TAC DESIGNATIONS (DESG)																
DESG	6300	T3P Designation Check Flight	B	E	A	1	(N*)	*						3.0				190

Enclosure (1)

VMR-1 PILOT T&R MATRIX

FUNCTIONAL CHECK FLIGHT (FCF)

STAGE	TRNG CODE	T&R DESCRIPTION	POI	DEVICE E	E	A/C	# OF A/C	CON	RE FLY	# OF ACAD	ACAD TIME	# OF SIM	SIM TIME	# OF FLTS	FLT TIME	PREREQUISITE	NOTES	CHAINING	EVENT CONV
DESG	6400	T2P Designation Check Flight	B,R	E	A	1		(N*)	*						3.0				290
DESG	6500	TAC Designation Check Flight	B,R	E	A	1		(N*)	*						3.0				390
		TOTAL DESG STAGE								0	0.0	0	0.0	3	9.0				
FCF	6600	FCF Training	B,R	E	A	1		D	*						4.0	5100			602
FCF	6601	FCF Evaluation	B,R	E	A	1		D	+						4.0	6600			603
		TOTAL FCF STAGE								0	0.0	0	0.0	2	8.0				
		RQD TOTAL (6000 PHASE)								7	20.5	2	6.0	8	21.0				
		TOTAL 5000,6000 STAGES								7	20.5	2	6.0	10	27.0				
		TOTAL 1000,2000,3000,4000,5000,6000 STAGES								11	28.5	17	66.0	23	70.0				

2.24   PILOT AND COPILOT CURRENCY MATRIX

TAC CURRENCY	REQUIREMENT TO REGAIN CURRENCY
OVER 30 DAYS SINCE LAST FLIGHT AS TAC OR COPILOT	FLY ONE FLIGHT (TRAINER OR MISSION)AS A COPILOT PRIOR TO FLYING AS A TAC
OVER 60 DAYS SINCE LAST FLIGHT AS TAC OR COPILOT	FLY ONE TRAINER AS A COPILOT WITH A TAC PRIOR TO FLYING AS A TAC
OVER 90 DAYS SINCE LAST FLIGHT AS TAC OR COPILOT	FLY ONE TRAINER AS A COPILOT WITH A TAC AND A NATOPS CHECK WITH AN IP
OVER 180 DAYS SINCE LAST FLIGHT AS TAC OR COPILOT	COMPLETE THE REFRESH SYLLABUS PER PARAGRAPH 102
OVER 24 MONTHS SINCE LAST FLIGHT AS TAC OR COPILOT*	FLY THE ENTIRE C-9B SYLLABUS BEGINNING WITH THE CORE SKILL INTRODUCTION PHASE*
COPILOT CURRENCY	REQUIREMENT TO REGAIN CURRENCY
OVER 60 DAYS SINCE LAST FLIGHT	FLY ONE TRAINER WITH A TAC
OVER 90 DAYS SINCE LAST FLIGHT	FLY ONE TRAINER WITH AN IP AND A NATOPS CHECK WITH AN IP
OVER 180 DAYS SINCE LAST FLIGHT	COMPLETE THE REFRESH SYLLABUS PER PARAGRAPH 102
OVER 24 MONTHS SINCE LAST FLIGHT	FLY THE ENTIRE C-9B SYLLABUS BEGINNING WITH THE CORE SKILL INTRODUCTION PHASE

CHAPTER 3

CREW CHIEF

3.0   INDIVIDUAL TRAINING AND READINESS REQUIREMENTS. This T&R syllabus is based on specific goals and performance standards designed to ensure individual proficiency in Core, Mission, and Core Plus Skills. The goal of this chapter is to develop individual and unit war fighting capabilities.

3.1   TRAINING PROGRESSION MODEL. This model represents the recommended training progression for the average C-9B Crew Chief. Units should use the model as a guide to generate individual training plans.

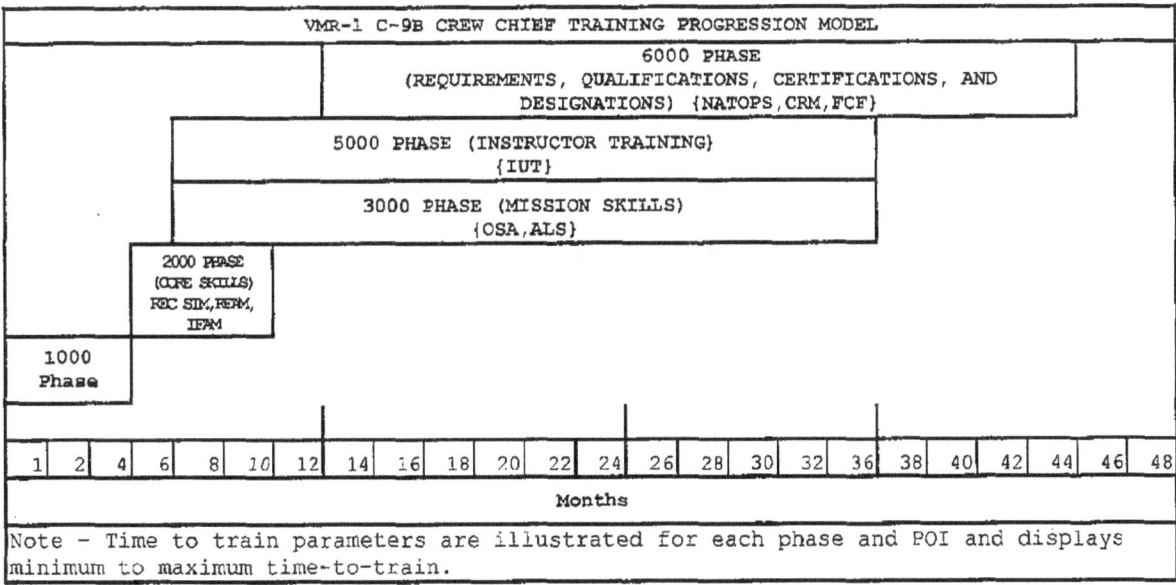

VMR-1 C-9B CREW CHIEF TRAINING PROGRESSION MODEL

6000 PHASE
(REQUIREMENTS, QUALIFICATIONS, CERTIFICATIONS, AND DESIGNATIONS) {NATOPS,CRM,FCF}

5000 PHASE (INSTRUCTOR TRAINING)
{IUT}

3000 PHASE (MISSION SKILLS)
{OSA,ALS}

2000 PHASE
(CORE SKILLS)
REC SIM,RFAM, IFAM

1000 Phase

| 1 | 2 | 4 | 6 | 8 | 10 | 12 | 14 | 16 | 18 | 20 | 22 | 24 | 26 | 28 | 30 | 32 | 36 | 38 | 40 | 42 | 44 | 46 | 48 |

Months

Note – Time to train parameters are illustrated for each phase and POI and displays minimum to maximum time-to-train.

3.2   ABBREVIATIONS

VMR-1 C-9B CREW CHIEF	
CORE/MISSION/CORE PLUS SKILL ABBREVIATIONS	
CORE SKILLS (2000 Phase)	
FAM	Familiarization
REC SIM	Recurrent Simulators
RFAM	Review Familiarization
IFAM	International Familiarization
MISSION SKILLS (3000 Phase)	
OSA	Operational Airlift Support
ALS	Air Logistics Support
INSTRUCTOR (5000 Phase)	
CCI	Crew Chief Instructor
CCE	Crew Chief NATOPS Evaluator
QUALIFICATIONS AND DESIGNATIONS (6000 Phase)	
ACAD	Academics
NTPS	NATOPS
EP	Emergency Procedures
DESG	Designation

NAVMC 3500.31A
22 Nov 11

3.3   DEFINITIONS

TERM	DEFINITION
Core Model	The Core Model is the basic foundation or standardized format by which all T&Rs are constructed. The Core Model provides the capability of quantifying both unit and individual training requirements and measuring readiness. This is accomplished by linking community Mission Statements, Mission Essential Task Lists, Output Standards, Core Skill Proficiency Requirements and Combat Leadership Matrices
Core Skill	Fundamental, environmental, or conditional capabilities required to perform basic functions. These basic functions serve as tactical enablers that allow crews to progress to the more complex Mission Skills. Primarily 2000 Phase events but may be introduced in the 1000 Phase.
Mission Skill	Mission Skills enable a unit to execute a specific MET. They are comprised of advanced event(s) that are focused on MET performance and draw upon the knowledge, aeronautical abilities, and situational awareness developed during Core Skill training. 3000 Phase events.
Core Plus Skill	Training events that can be theater specific or that have a low likelihood of occurrence. They may be fundamental, environmental, or conditional capabilities required to perform basic functions. 4000 Phase events.
Core Plus Mission	Training events that can be theater specific or that have a low likelihood of occurrence. They are comprised of advanced event(s) that are focused on Core Plus MET performance and draw upon the knowledge, aeronautical abilities, and situational awareness. 4000 Phase events.
Core Skill Proficiency (CSP)	CSP is a measure of training completion for 2000 Phase events. CSP is attained by executing all events listed in the Attain Table for each Core Skill. The individual must be simultaneously proficient in all events within that Core Skill to attain CSP.
Mission Skill Proficiency (MSP)	MSP is a measure of training completion for 3000 Phase events. MSP is attained by executing all events listed in the Attain Table for each Mission Skill. The individual must be simultaneously proficient in all events within that Mission Skill to attain MSP. MSP is directly related to Training Readiness.
Core Plus Skill Proficiency (CPSP)	CPSP is a measure of training completion for 4000 Phase "Skill" events. CPSP is attained by executing all events listed in the Attain Table for each Core Plus Skill. The individual must be simultaneously proficient in all events within that Core Plus Skill to attain CPSP
Core Plus Mission Proficiency (CPMP)	CPMP is a measure of training completion for 4000 Phase "Mission" events. CPMP is attained by executing all events listed in the Attain Table for each Core Plus Mission. The individual must be simultaneously proficient in all events within that Core Plus Mission to attain CPMP

3.4   INDIVIDUAL CORE/MISSION/CORE PLUS SKILL PROFICIENCY REQUIREMENTS

3.4.1   Management of individual CSP/MSP/CPSP/CPMP serves as the foundation for developing proficiency requirements in DRRS.

3.4.2   Individual CSP is a "Yes/No" status assigned to an individual by Core Skill. When an individual attains and maintains CSP in a Core Skill, the individual counts towards CMMR Unit CSP requirements for that Core Skill.

3.4.3   Proficiency is attained by individual Core/Mission/Core Plus Skill and the training events to be executed within that skill set are determined by POI assignment (Basic, Transition, Conversion, Series Conversion, or Refresher).

3.4.4   Once proficiency has been attained by Core/Mission/Core Plus Skill (by any POI assignment) then the individual maintains proficiency by executing those events within the maintain column. An individual maintains proficiency by individual Core/Mission/Core Plus Skill.

Note
Individuals may be attaining proficiency
in some Core/Mission/Core Plus Skills

while maintaining proficiency in other
Core/Mission/Core Plus Skills.

3.4.5   Once proficiency has been attained, should one lose proficiency in
an event in the maintain column, proficiency can be attained by demonstrating
proficiency in the event which was delinquent. Should an individual lose
proficiency in all events in the maintain column by Core/Mission/Core Plus
Skill, the individual will be assigned to the refresher POI for that
Core/Mission/Core Plus Skill. To regain proficiency for that
Core/Mission/Core Plus Skill the individual must demonstrate proficiency in
all R-coded events for that Core/Mission/Core Plus Skill.

VMR-1 C-9B CREW CHIEF						
ATTAIN AND MAINTAIN CORE/MISSION/CORE PLUS PROFICIENCY MATRIX BY POI						
CORE SKILL (2000 Phase)						
ATTAIN PROFICIENCY				MAINTAIN PROFICIENCY		
BASIC POI		REFRESHER POI		MAINTAIN POI		
RECSIM	S2100R	RECSIM	S2100R	RECSIM		S2100R
	S2101R		S2101R			S2101R
	S2102R		S2102R			S2102R
RFAM	2200	RFAM		RFAM		
	2201					
	2202					
	2203					
	2204R		2204R			
	2205R		2205R			2205R
IFAM	2301	IFAM	2301R	IFAM		2301R
MISSION SKILL (3000 Phase)						
ATTAIN PROFICIENCY				MAINTAIN PROFICIENCY		
BASIC POI		REFRESHER POI		MAINTAIN POI		
OSA	3100R	OSA	3100R	OSA		3100R
ALS	3200R	ALS	3200R	ALS		3200R
S prefix and blue font = flown in simulator						
R suffix and Grey highlight = R-coded "Refresher" event						

3.5   CERTIFICATION, QUALIFICATION AND DESIGNATION TABLES. The tables
below delineate T&R events required to be completed to attain proficiency,
initial qualifications and designations. In addition to event requirements,
all required stage lectures, briefs, squadron training, prerequisites, and
other criteria shall be completed prior to completing final events.
Certification, qualification and designation letters signed by the Commanding
Officer shall be placed in individual NATOPS jackets. Loss of proficiency in
all qualification events causes the associated qualification to be lost.
Regaining a qualification requires completing all R-coded syllabus events
associated with that qualification.

3.5.1   INSTRUCTOR DESIGNATIONS

VMR-1 C-9B CREW CHIEF	
INSTRUCTOR DESIGNATIONS (5000 Phase)	
INSTRUCTOR DESIGNATION	EVENTS
CC ASSISTANT NATOPS INSTRUCTOR (CC NI/ANI)	6200,5100,5101
CC NATOPS EVALUATOR/INSTRUCTOR (CC NE)	6200,5100,5101,5102

3.5.2   REQUIREMENTS, CERTIFICATIONS, QUALIFICATIONS, AND DESIGNATIONS

3.5.2.1 The tables below delineate T&R events required to be completed to
attain initial qualifications and designations. All stage lectures, briefs,
squadron training, prerequisites, and open and closed book NATOPS exams shall

be complete and graded prior to completing evaluation flights. Qualification and designation letters signed by the Commanding Officer shall be placed in individual NATOPS jackets.

VMR-1 C-9B CREW CHIEF	
REQUIREMENTS, CERTIFICATIONS, QUALIFICATIONS, AND DESIGNATIONS (R,C,Q,& D) [6000 Phase]	
R,C,Q,& D	EVENTS
QUALIFICATIONS	
NATOPS	6000,6001,6002,6100
CRM	6005,6101
DESIGNATIONS	
CC	6200

3.6   VMR-1 C-9B CREW CHIEF PROGRAMS OF INSTRUCTION (POI). These tables reflect average time-to-train versus the minimum to maximum time-to-train parameters in the Training Progression Model.

3.6.1   Basic POI. A Basic Crew Chief shall be defined as a C-9B Crew Chief who obtains all Crew Chief training aboard the C-9B. Prior to commencing this POI, an individual shall be designated as a C-9B 2nd Loadmaster (2LM), should have flown 50 hours as a 2LM, and shall be recommended by the Squadron Standardization Board and approved by the Squadron CO. All decisions as to POI eligibility rest with the Commanding Officer.

VMR-1 C-9B CREW CHIEF		
Basic POI		
Weeks	Phase of Instruction	Unit
1	Water survival/flight physiology*	NAWSTP
2-6	C-9B 2LM syllabus	VMR-1
As Required	Ground training	VMR-1
7-23	Core Skill Introduction (1000 Phase)	VMR-1
24-48	Core Skill (2000 Phase)	VMR 1
24-48	Mission Skill (3000 Phase)	VMR-1
* Required only if NAWSTP swim qualification has expired.		

3.6.2   Refresher POI. The CCUI must have flown in the capacity as a C-9B Crew Chief during the previous two years in order to be eligible for this Refresher POI. The CCUI shall have been recommended by the Squadron Standardization Board and approved by the Commanding Officer prior to commencing this Refresher POI. All decisions as to POI eligibility rest with the Commanding Officer.

VMR-1 C-9B CREW CHIEF		
Refresher POI		
Weeks	Phase of Instruction	Unit
1	Water survival/flight physiology *	NAWSTP
2-3	Core Introduction (1000 Phase)	VMR-1
4	Core Skill (2000 Phase)	VMR-1
4	Mission Skill (3000 Phase)	VMR-1
• Required only if NAWSTP swim qualification is expired.		

3.6.3   POI FOR INSTRUCTOR CREW CHIEF UNDER TRAINING (CCIUT). The CCIUT shall have been recommended by the Squadron Standardization Board and approved by the Commanding Officer prior to commencing this POI. All decisions as to POI eligibility rest with the Commanding Officer.

VMR-1 C-9B CREW CHIEF		
Instructor POI		
Weeks	Phase of Instruction	Unit
1-2	CC Instructor Training	VMR-1
As Required	CC NATOPS Evaluator Training	VMR-1

3.7   SYLLABUS NOTES

3.7.1   Environmental Conditions Matrix

Environmental Conditions	
Code	Meaning
D	Shall be flown during hours of daylight: (by exception - there is no use of a symbol)
N*	Shall be flown during hours of darkness must be flown unaided
(N*)	May be flown during hours of darkness - If flown during hours of darkness must be flown unaided
Note - If the event is to be flown in the simulator the Simulator Instructor shall set the desired environmental conditions for the event.	

3.7.2   Device Matrix

DEVICE (Aviation Flying)	
Symbol	Meaning
A	Flown in aircraft
A/S	Aircraft preferred may be flown in Simulator
S	Flown in simulator
S/A	Simulator preferred may be flown in aircraft
CBT	Computer Based Training
Note - If the event is to be flown in the simulator the Simulator Instructor shall set the desired environmental conditions for the event.	

3.7.3   Program of Instruction Matrix

PROGRAM OF INSTRUCTION MATRIX			
Program of Instruction (POI)	Symbol	Aviation Flying	Aviation Ground
Basic	B	Initial MOS/skill training	Initial MOS training
Refresher	R	DIFDEN to DIFOPS in same T/M/S	Return to community from non (MOS/Skill) associated tour

3.7.4   Event Terms

EVENT TERMS	
TERM	DESCRIPTION
Discuss	An explanation of systems, procedures, or maneuvers during the brief, in flight, or post flight. Student is responsible for knowledge of procedures.
Demonstrate	The description and performance of a particular maneuver/event by the instructor, observed by the CCUI/student. The CCUI/student is responsible for knowledge of the procedures prior to the demonstration of a required maneuver/student.
Introduce	The instructor may demonstrate a procedure or maneuver to a student, or may coach the CCUI through the maneuver without demonstration. The CCUI performs the procedures or maneuver with coaching as necessary. The CCUI is responsible for knowledge of the procedures.
Practice	The performance of a maneuver or procedure by the CCUI/student that may have been previously introduced in order to attain a specified level of performance.
Review	Demonstrated proficiency of a maneuver by the CCUI/student.
Evaluate	Any flight designed to evaluate aircrew standardization that does not fit another category such as SARCK, HACCK, T2PCK, etc.
E-Coded	This term means that documentation (ATF) is required each time the event is logged. Requires evaluation by a certified standardization instructor (NATOPS I, WTI, INST Evaluator etc.)

3.8   CORE SKILL INTRODUCTION FRS ACADEMIC PHASE (0000 Phase). There are no 0000 Phase events in the C-9B T&R manual. However, the squadron training listed below is required.

3.8.1   The following ground training is intended for Basic Crew Chief students during initial qualification. Refresher Crew Chiefs are exempt from these ground training events. The Crew Chief student is required to have been previously designated as a 2LM on the C-9B aircraft prior to assignment to the Crew Chief syllabus. However, the ground training described below may be conducted concurrently with the 2LM syllabus. This ground training should be complete prior to commencing DESG-6200.

3.8.1.1 Professional School Training

Activity	Location
Power plants and Airframes School	Fort Worth JRB
APU Triumph/Raytheon*	Fort Worth JRB/Phoenix, AZ

3.8.1.2 Squadron Ground Training
General aircraft description
Required support equipment
Review of C-9B phase inspection
JT-8D engine low power turn qualification
C-9B Plane Captain qualification
C-9B APU qualification
C-9B tow qualification
C-9B tire/wheel qualification
LOX qualification
Aircraft emergency systems review
Personal flying equipment requirements review

3.9   CORE SKILL INTRODUCTION PHASE (1000). The Core Skill Introduction Phase is designed to familiarize the CCUI with C-9B ground servicing, normal procedures, CRM, systems operation and limitations, and emergency procedures.

3.10   CORE SKILL INTRODUCTION STAGES (1000)

PARAGRAPH	STAGE
3.10.1	Simulation Flights (SIM)
3.10.2	Familiarization Flights

3.10.1   SIMULATION FLIGHTS (Initial) (SIM)

3.10.1.1 Purpose. The current prescribed C-9B flight simulator course is designed to familiarize the CCUI with C-9B normal cockpit procedures, crew coordination, systems operations and limitations, emergency procedures and to introduce instrument flight procedures.

3.10.1.2 General. CCUIs shall attend the simulator training with two Initial or Refresher pilots. While it is strongly encouraged, attendance at initial simulator training is not mandatory prior to initial designation as a C-9B Crew Chief. However, attendance is mandatory within twelve months of beginning the Crew Chief syllabus. Refresher simulator training is considered sufficient for a CCUIs first simulator exposure. However, every effort should be made to send the CCUI or newly-designated Crew Chief to Initial simulator training.

3.10.1.2 Crew Requirements. T3P, T2P, CCUI

SIM-1100   4.0   *   B   (N*)   S(No Motion)   1 C-9B

    Goal. Per current contract.

    Requirement. Per current contract.

    Performance Standard. Per current contract.

SIM-1101   4.0   *   B   (N*)   S(No Motion)   1 C-9B

    Goal. Per current contract.

    Requirement. Per current contract.

    Performance Standard. Per current contract.

    Prerequisite. SIM-1100

SIM-1102   4.0   *   B   (N*)   S(No Motion)   1 C-9B

    Goal. Per current contract.

    Requirement. Per current contract.

    Performance Standard. Per current contract.

    Prerequisite. SIM-1101

SIM-1103   4.0   *   B   (N*)   S(No Motion)   1 C-9B

    Goal. Per current contract.

    Requirement. Per current contract.

    Performance Standard. Per current contract.

    Prerequisite. SIM-1102

SIM-1104   4.0   *   B   (N*)   S   1 C-9B

    Goal. Per current contract.

    Requirement. Per current contract.

    Performance Standard. Per current contract.

    Prerequisite. SIM-1103

SIM-1105   4.0   *   B   (N*)   S   1 C-9B

    Goal. Per current contract.

    Requirement. Per current contract.

    Performance Standard. Per current contract.

    Prerequisite. SIM-1104

SIM-1106   4.0   *   B   (N*)   S   1 C-9B

    Goal. Per current contract.

    Requirement. Per current contract.

    Performance Standard. Per current contract.

    Prerequisite. SIM-1105

SIM-1107   4.0   *   B   (N*)   S   1 C-9B

    Goal. Per current contract.

    Requirement. Per current contract.

    Performance Standard. Per current contract.

    Prerequisite. SIM-1106

SIM-1108   4.0   *   B   (N*)   S   1 C-9B

    Goal. Per current contract.

    Requirement. Per current contract.

    Performance Standard. Per current contract.

    Prerequisite. SIM-1107

SIM-1109   4.0   *   B   (N*)   S   1 C-9B

    Goal. Per current contract.
    Requirement. Per current contract.
    Performance Standard. Per current contract.
    Prerequisite. SIM-1108

SIM-1110   4.0   *   B   (N*)   S   1 C-9B

    Goal. Per current contract.
    Requirement. Per current contract.
    Performance Standard. Per current contract.
    Prerequisite. SIM-1109

SIM-1111   4.0   *   B   (N*)   S   1 C-9B

    Goal. Per current contract.
    Requirement. Per current contract.
    Performance Standard. Per current contract.

    Prerequisite. SIM-1110

3.10.2   FAMILIARIZATION FLIGHTS (FAM)

3.10.2.1 Purpose. Familiarize the CCUI with the C-9B aircraft. Instruction will emphasize adherence to NATOPS procedures, operation of aircraft systems, and aircraft servicing.

3.10.2.2 General. Training may be accomplished aboard either training or operational missions.

3.10.2.3 Crew Requirements. TAC, T2P or T3P, CCI, CCUI (If training on an operational mission full mission crew required)

FAM-1300   3.0   *   B   (N*)   A   1 C-9B

    Goal. Introduce Auxiliary Power Unit (APU), daily, turnaround, pre/post-flight inspections, and general servicing requirements.
    Requirement
      Discuss

        Review NATOPS procedures and applicable maintenance manuals associated with the (APU)
        Daily and turnaround inspection
        Preflight and postflight inspection
        General servicing requirements

      Demonstrate/Introduce

        Emergency procedures
        Jump seat duties
        Checklist procedures
        CRM
        NATOPS procedures and applicable maintenance manuals associated with the (APU)
        Daily/post flight inspection
        Servicing and turnaround of engine system

Review

    Previously covered material as necessary

Performance Standard

    Demonstrate a basic understanding of applicable systems/ inspections/procedures in accordance with (IAW) NATOPS, SOP, and applicable Maintenance Manuals.

    Recite all bold face emergency procedures before occupying the CC jump seat for take-off and landings.

Prerequisite. Previously designated as a C-9B 2LM.

FAM-1301   3.0   *   B   (N*)   A   1 C-9B

Goal. Introduce emergency procedures (all types).

Requirement

    Discuss

        Any memorized bold face emergency procedure items in the C-9B NATOPS Flight Manual
        Any C-9B operation limitations
        Fire warning operation and emergency procedures
        Operation following decompression
        Aircraft lighting
        Engine system and emergency procedures

    Demonstrate/Introduce/Practice

        Any memorized bold face emergency procedure items in the C-9B NATOPS Flight Manual
        Any C-9B operation limitations

    Review

        Previously covered material as necessary

Performance Standard

    Demonstrate a basic understanding of applicable systems/inspections/procedures (IAW) NATOPS, SOP, and applicable maintenance manuals.

    Recite all bold face emergency procedures before occupying the Crew Chief jump seat for take-off and landings.

Prerequisite. FAM-1300

FAM-1302   3.0   *   B   (N*)   A   1 C-9B

Goal. Review all emergency procedures and introduce AC and DC electrical systems and fuel systems.

Requirement

    Discuss

        Discuss NATOPS procedures and applicable maintenance manuals associated with the AC and DC electrical systems and fuel systems
        Any memorized bold face emergency procedure items in the C-9B NATOPS Flight Manual
        Any C-9B operation limitations

    Demonstrate/Introduce/Practice

        NATOPS procedures and applicable maintenance manuals associated with the AC and DC electrical systems and fuel systems
        Electrical and fuel system emergency procedures

Review

    Previously covered material as necessary
    Any memorized bold face emergency procedure items in the C-9B
    NATOPS Flight Manual
    Any C-9B operation limitations

Performance Standard

    Demonstrate a basic understanding of applicable
    systems/inspections/procedures (IAW) NATOPS, SOP, and applicable
    maintenance manuals.

    Recite all bold face emergency procedures before occupying the
    Crew Chief jump seat for take-off and landings.

Prerequisite. FAM-1301

FAM-1303   3.0   *   B   (N*)   A   1 C-9B

    Goal. Review all emergency procedures and introduce hydraulic
    system and landing gear.

    Requirement

    Discuss

        Discuss NATOPS procedures and applicable maintenance manuals
        associated with the hydraulic and landing gear systems
        Any memorized bold face emergency procedure items in the C-9B
        NATOPS Flight Manual
        Any C-9B operation limitations

    Demonstrate/Introduce/Practice

        NATOPS procedures and applicable maintenance manuals associated
        with the hydraulic systems and landing gear systems
        Hydraulic and landing gear emergency procedures

    Review

        Previously covered material as necessary
        Any memorized bold face emergency procedure items in the C-9B
        NATOPS Flight Manual
        Any C-9B operation limitations

    Performance Standard

        Demonstrate a basic understanding of applicable
        systems/inspections/procedures (IAW) NATOPS, SOP, and applicable
        maintenance manuals.

        Recite all bold face emergency procedures with no deficiencies.

    Prerequisite. FAM-1302

FAM-1304   3.0   *   B   (N*)   A   1 C-9B

    Goal. Review all emergency procedures and introduce flight control and
    pneumatic systems.

    Requirement

    Discuss

        Discuss NATOPS procedures and applicable maintenance manuals
        associated with the flight control and pneumatic systems
        Any memorized bold face emergency procedure items in the C-9B
        NATOPS Flight Manual
        Any C-9B operation limitations

Demonstrate/Introduce/Practice

> NATOPS procedures and applicable maintenance manuals associated
> with the flight control and pneumatic systems
> Flight control and pneumatic emergency procedures

Review

> Previously covered material as necessary
> Any memorized bold face emergency procedure items in the C-9B
> NATOPS Flight Manual
> Any C-9B operation limitations

Performance Standard

> Demonstrate a basic understanding of applicable systems/
> inspections/procedures (IAW) NATOPS, SOP, and applicable
> Maintenance Manuals.
>
> Recite all Bold Face emergency procedure with no deficiencies.

Prerequisite. FAM-1303

FAM-1305   3.0   *   B   (N*)   A   1 C-9B

Goal. Review all emergency procedures and introduce fire
warning/protection and oxygen systems.

Requirement

Discuss

> Discuss NATOPS procedures and applicable maintenance manuals
> associated with the fire warning/protection and oxygen systems
> Any memorized bold face emergency procedure items in the C-9B
> NATOPS Flight Manual
> Any C-9B operation limitations

Demonstrate/Introduce/Practice

> NATOPS procedures and applicable maintenance manuals associated
> with the fire warning/protection and oxygen systems

Review

> Previously covered material as necessary
> Any memorized bold face emergency procedure items in the C-9B
> NATOPS Flight Manual
> Any C-9B operation limitations

Performance Standard

> Demonstrate a basic understanding of applicable systems/
> inspections/procedures (IAW) NATOPS, SOP, and applicable
> Maintenance Manuals.
>
> Recite all bold face emergency procedures with no deficiencies.

Prerequisite. FAM-1304

FAM-1306   3.0   *   B,R   E   (N*)   A   1 C-9B

Goal. Evaluate CCUI progress in the Crew Chief syllabus.

Requirement

Discuss

> All previously covered material
> All memorized bold face emergency procedure items in the C-9B
> NATOPS Flight Manual
> All C-9B operation limitations

Review

> Previously covered material as necessary

All memorized bold face emergency procedure items in the C-9B
NATOPS Flight Manual
All C-9B operation limitations

Performance Standard

Demonstrate a basic understanding of all systems/
inspections/procedures (IAW) NATOPS, SOP, and applicable
Maintenance Manuals.
Recite all bold face emergency procedures with no deficiencies.
Demonstrate knowledge of aircraft and engine limitations with
minimal deficiencies

Prerequisite. FAM-1305

3.11 CORE SKILL PHASE (2000)

3.11.1 General. This phase introduces the CCUI to night responsibilities
and review of all systems and International/Transoceanic flight to build
confidence and competence.

3.12 CORE SKILL INTRODUCTION STAGES (2000)

PARAGRAPH	STAGE
3.12.1	Recurrent/Refresher Simulators (RECSIM)
3.12.2	Review Familiarization (RFAM)
3.12.3	International Familiarization (IFAM)

3.12.1 RECURRENT/REFRESHER SIMULATOR TRAINING (RECSIM)

3.12.1.1 Purpose. Review C-9B normal cockpit procedures, CRM, systems
operation and limitations, emergency procedures, and instrument flight
procedures.

3.12.1.2 General. Attendance at recurrent/refresher simulator training is
required prior to re-designation as a Crew Chief, however it is not a
prerequisite to begin the Refresher Crew Chief syllabus. The Crew Chief
simulator re-fly interval is recommended every 12-18 months, not to exceed 24
months.

3.12.1.3 Crew Requirements. Per current contract

RECSIM-2100 4.0   730   B,R   (N*)   S   1 C-9B

Goal. Per current contract.
Requirement. Per current contract.
Performance Standard. Per current contract.

RECSIM-2101 4.0   730   B,R   (N*)   S   1 C-9B

Goal. Per current contract.
Requirement. Per current contract.
Performance Standard. Per current contract.
Prerequisite. REFSIM-2100

RECSIM-2102 4.0   730   B,R,M   (N*)   S   1 C-9B

Goal. Per current contract.
Requirement. Per current contract.
Performance Standard. Per current contract.

Prerequisite. REFSIM-2101

3.12.2 Review Familiarization (RFAM)

3.12.2.1 Purpose. Review of all aircraft systems and Crew Chief responsibilities in preparation for designation as a C-9B Crew Chief.

3.12.2.2 Crew Requirements. TAC, T2P or T3P, CCI, CCUI (If accomplished on a mission flight full mission crew must be present)

RFAM-2200   5.0   *   B   N*   A   1 C-9B

> Goal. Review emergency procedures (all types) and introduce night procedures.
>
> Requirement
>
>> Discuss
>>
>>> Any memorized bold face emergency procedure items in the C-9B NATOPS Flight Manual
>>> Any C-9B operation limitations
>>> Fire warning operation and Emergency Procedures
>>> Operation following decompression
>>> Aircraft Lighting
>>> Engine system and emergency procedures
>>> Crew Chief responsibilities during night operations
>>
>> Demonstrate/Introduce/Practice
>>
>>> Crew chief responsibilities during night operations
>>
>> Review
>>
>>> Previously covered material as necessary
>
> Performance Standard. Demonstrate an increase in knowledge and retention of information covered in 1300 series codes regarding applicable systems and procedures IAW NATOPS, SOP, and applicable maintenance manuals.
>
> Prerequisite. FAM-1306

RFAM-2201   5.0   *   B   N*   A   1 C-9B

> Goal. Review AC/DC electrical systems, fuel system, and hydraulic system. Review night operations.
>
> Requirement
>
>> Discuss
>>
>>> AC/DC electrical systems
>>> Fuel system
>>> Hydraulic system
>>> Review night operations
>>> Previously covered material as necessary
>>
>> Review
>>
>>> AC/DC electrical systems and associated emergency procedures
>>> Fuel system and associated emergency procedures
>>> Hydraulic system and associated emergency procedures
>>> Review night operations
>>> Previously covered material as necessary
>
> Performance Standard. Demonstrate an increase in knowledge and retention of information covered in 1300 series codes regarding applicable systems and procedures IAW NATOPS, SOP, and applicable maintenance manuals.
>
> Prerequisite. RFAM-2200

RFAM-2202   5.0   *   B   (N*)   A   1 C-9B

    Goal. Review landing gear and flight control systems.

    Requirement

        Discuss

            Landing gear system
            Flight controls
            Previously covered material as necessary

        Review

            Landing gear system and associated emergency procedures
            Flight Controls and associated emergency procedures
            Previously covered material as necessary

    Performance Standard. Demonstrate an increase in knowledge and
retention of information covered in 1300 series codes regarding applicable
systems and procedures IAW NATOPS, SOP, and applicable maintenance manuals.

    Prerequisite. FAM-1306

RFAM-2203   5.0   *   B   (N*)   A   1 C-9B

    Goal. Review pneumatic, fire warning/protection, and oxygen systems.

    Requirement

        Discuss

            Pneumatic system
            Fire warning/protection
            Oxygen system
            Previously covered material as necessary

        Review

            Pneumatic system and associated emergency procedures fire
            warning/protection
            Oxygen system
            Previously covered material as necessary

    Performance Standard. Demonstrate an increase in knowledge and
retention of information covered in 1300 series codes regarding applicable
systems and procedures IAW NATOPS, SOP, and applicable maintenance manuals.

    Prerequisite. RFAM-2202

RFAM-2204   5.0   *   B,R   E   (N*)   A   1 C-9B

    Goal. CCUI Progress Check.

    Requirement

        Discuss

            Previously covered material as necessary

        Review/Evaluate

            Previously covered material as necessary

    Performance Standard

            Demonstrate an intermediate level of understanding of applicable
            systems/inspections/procedures IAW NATOPS, SOP, and applicable
            maintenance manuals.

            Recite all Bold Face emergency procedures with no deficiencies.

            Demonstrate knowledge of aircraft and engine limitations with no
            deficiencies.

    Prerequisite. RFAM-2201, RFAM-2203

RFAM-2205   4.0   90   B,R,M   (N*)   A   1 C-9B

    Goal. Review all 1000/2000 series events. This code will be used to log trainer and FCF flights for qualified Crew Chiefs.

    Requirement
       Discuss
          All previously covered material from the 1000/2000 series
       Review
          All previously covered material from the 1000/2000 series
    Performance Standard
       Demonstrate a high level of understanding of applicable systems/inspections/procedures IAW NATOPS, SOP, and applicable maintenance manuals.
       Recite all bold face emergency procedures with no deficiencies.
       Demonstrate knowledge of aircraft and engine limitations with no deficiencies.
    Prerequisite. RFAM-2204

3.12.3   International Familiarization (IFAM)

3.12.3.1 Purpose. Ensure the CCUI has a complete understanding of Crew Chief responsibilities on International/Trans Oceanic flights.

3.12.3.2 Crew Requirements. TAC, T2P or T3P, CCI, CCUI (If accomplished on a mission flight full mission crew must be present)

IFAM-2301   5.0   365   B,R,M   (N*)   A   1 C-9B

    Goal. CCUI will be instructed on responsibilities of a Crew Chief on an International/Transoceanic flight. Qualified CCs will use this code for update of International/Transoceanic flights.

    Exception. May be conducted transcontinental if trans Oceanic flight has been conducted previously in syllabus.

    Requirement
       Discuss
          CC responsibilities on an International/Transoceanic flight
          Previously covered material as necessary
       Introduce/Review
          CC responsibilities on an International/Transoceanic flight
          Previously covered material as necessary
    Performance Standard. Demonstrate understanding of Crew Chief responsibilities on a long-range, overwater, or extended flight with regard to special servicing and/or logistical requirements IAW NATOPS, SOP, and applicable Maintenance Manuals.
    Prerequisite. FAM-1306

3.13   MISSION SKILLS PHASE (3000)

3.13.1   General. The Mission Skill Phase is designed to familiarize the CCUI with the unique missions and challenges associated with the VMR-1, C-9B. Mission Skills are designed to fulfill the requirements of the C-9B Mission Essential Task List as defined by the associated Marine Corps Task (MCT).

3.14   MISSION SKILL STAGES (3000)

PARAGRAPH	STAGE
3.14.1	Operational Support Airlift (OSA)
3.14.2	Air Logistics Support (ALS)

3.14.1 Operational Support Airlift (OSA)

3.14.1.1 Purpose. This event is designed to fulfill the requirement set in MCT 1.3.4.1.2, conduct OSA.

3.14.1.2 General. It is understood that many missions will be a combination of both passenger and cargo transportation and both codes will be used when filling out the NAVFLIR. Both codes are made available for flights that clearly fall into a single category.

3.14.1.3 Crew Requirement. Full mission crew (as required).

OSA-3100   5.0   180   B,R,M   (N*)   A   1   C-9B

    Goal. Introduce the CCUI to the JOSAC passenger mission or provide continued update to the skills of the CC while performing the passenger mission. Initial logging of this code will be accomplished on the first passenger mission during the Core Skills Stage (2000). Qualified Crew Chiefs will use this code on all subsequent OSA missions.

    Requirement

        Discuss

            Any specific considerations or requirements for conducting JOSAC, ASM, or other passenger missions.

        Review

            Previously covered material as necessary.

    Performance Standard. IAW NATOPS

    Prerequisite. FAM-1306

3.14.2 Air Logistics Support (ALS) .

3.14.2.1 Purpose. This event is designed to fulfill the requirement set in MMC 4.3.8, conduct ALS.

3.14.2.2 General. It is understood that many missions will be a combination of both passenger and cargo transportation and both codes will be used when filling out the NAVFLIR. Both codes are made available for flights that clearly fall into a single category.

3.14.2.3 Crew Requirement. Full mission crew (as required).

ALS-3200   5.0   180   B,R,M   (N*)   A   1   C-9B

    Goal. Introduce the CCUI to the C-9B cargo mission or provide continued update to the skills used while performing the cargo mission. Initial logging of this code will be accomplished on the first cargo mission during the Core Skills Stage (2000). Qualified Crew Chiefs will use this code on all subsequent ALS missions.

    Requirement

        Discuss

            Any specific considerations or requirements for conducting cargo missions.

        Review

            Previously covered material as necessary.

Performance Standard. IAW NATOPS
Prerequisite. FAM-1306

3.15   CORE PLUS SKILL PHASE (4000)

3.15.1   General. There is no Core Plus Skill Phase in the C-9B T&R.

3.16   CORE PLUS SKILL STAGES (4000)

3.16.1   General. There are no 4000 level events in the C-9B T&R.

3.17   INSTRUCTOR TRAINING PHASE (5000)

3.17.1   General. The instructor training phase is designed to provide the Squadron with a cadre of qualified instructors needed to ensure quality training at all times.

PARAGRAPH	STAGE
3.18.1	Instruction Under Training (IUT)

3.18.1   Instructor Under Training (IUT)

3.18.1.1 Purpose. Develop qualified instructor Crew Chiefs with the ability to teach all phases of C-9B flight and mission requirements.

3.18.1.2 General. Crew Chief Instructors will be designated as either NATOPS Instructor (NI) or Assistant NATOPS Instructor (ANI). A NI may instruct and designate an ANI but a NATOPS Evaluator (NE) shall evaluate and designate a NI. In addition to basic Crew Chief requirements, the IUT will have the following schools and certifications:

Crew Resource Management (CRM) Facilitator Course
APU Instructor Certification
Engine Low-power Run-up Instructor Certification

3.18.1.2 Crew Requirements. TAC, T2P or T3P, CCE/CCI, CCIUT, CCUI

IUT-5100   3.0   *   B   (N*)   A   1 C-9B

    Goal. Instruction introduction.
    Requirement
       Brief/Discuss
          Conduct of training flight
          Instructional techniques
       Review
          The CCIUT shall observe a CCE/CCI instruct a CCUI on a syllabus flight. The CCE/CCI shall demonstrate emphasis upon evaluating the CCUI's knowledge of aircraft systems, emergency procedures, and CC responsibilities.
    Performance Standard. CCIUT shall have a solid knowledge of aircraft and CC responsibilities during all aspects of ground and flight operations.
    Prerequisite. DESG-6200

IUT-5101   3.0   *   B   E   (N*)   A   1 C-9B

> Goal. Qualify a CC as a CCI (ANI) or upgrade an ANI to NI.
>
> Requirement
>
>> Discuss
>>
>>> Conduct of evaluation flight
>>> Any CC ground/flight responsibility and how that is taught to a CCUI
>>
>> Review
>>
>>> The CCIUT shall perform all duties of a CCI on a flight with a CCUI while being evaluated by a CCE/CCI.
>
> Performance Standard. CCIUT shall demonstrate the requisite maturity, instructional ability, and standardization expected of a CCI.
>
> Prerequisite. IUT-5100

IUT-5102   3.0   *   B,R,M   E   (N*)   A   1 C-9B

> Goal. Qualify the CCI as a CCE.
>
> Requirement
>
>> Discuss
>>
>>> Conduct of evaluation flight
>>> Responsibilities of the CCE
>>
>> Review
>>
>>> The CCI shall be evaluated by a CCE NATOPS Evaluator while instructing a CCUI. The CCI being evaluated must display the maturity, integrity, and knowledge of the aircraft required to conduct a NATOPS evaluation.
>
> Performance Standard. CCI shall demonstrate the requisite maturity, instructional ability, and standardization expected of a CCE.
>
> Prerequisite. IUT-5101

3.19   REQUIREMENTS, CERTIFICATIONS, QUALIFICATIONS, AND DESIGNATIONS (RCQD) PHASE (6000)

3.19.1   General. The 6000 phase encompasses the events required to maintain currency with all certifications, qualifications, and designations.

3.20   REQUIREMENTS, CERTIFICATIONS, QUALIFICATIONS, AND DESIGNATIONS (RCQD) STAGES (6000)

PARAGRAPH	STAGE
3.21.1	Academics (ACAD)
3.21.2	NATOPS Evaluations (NTPS)
3.21.3	Designations (DESG)

3.21.1   Academics (ACAD)

3.21.1.1 Purpose. To complete the academic requirements for subsequent annual evaluation flights.

ACAD-6000   4.0   365   B,R,M   E

> Goal. The NATOPS Open Book examination shall consist of, but not be limited to the question bank. The purpose of the open book examination

is to evaluate the Crew Chief's knowledge of the appropriate publications and the aircraft.

Performance Standard. Achieve a minimum score of 3.5 on the Open Book examination.

ACAD-6001   2.0   365   B,R,M   E

Goal. The purpose of the NATOPS closed book examination is to evaluate the Crew Chief's knowledge of the concerning normal/emergency procedures and aircraft limitations.

Performance Standard. Achieve a minimum score of 3.3 on the closed book examination.

Prerequisite. ACAD-6000

ACAD-6002   2.0   365   B,R,M   E

Goal. The NATOPS Oral Examination shall consist of, but not be limited to the question bank. The instructor may draw upon their experience to propose questions of a direct and positive manner and in no way be opinionated to evaluate the Crew Chief's knowledge of the concerning normal/emergency procedures, aircraft limitations, and performance. May be conducted in conjunction with DESG-6200 or NTPS-6100.

Performance Standard. Achieve a minimum grade of qualified on the oral examination.

Prerequisite. ACAD-6000 and ACAD-6001 within 60 days preceding this event.

ACAD-6005   2.0   365   B,R,M   E

Goal. CRM ground instruction in accordance with applicable directives and instructions.

Performance Standard. Demonstrate satisfactory knowledge of CRM principles and their application.

ACAD-6006   1.0   30   B,R,M   E

Goal. Monthly emergency procedures exam.

Requirement. Conduct a monthly emergency procedures exam per NAVMC 3500.14.

Performance Standard. Pass the Monthly Emergency Procedures Exam.

ACAD-6007   1.0   90   B,R,M   (N*)   E   S/A   1 C-9B

Goal. Emergency Procedure Review.

Requirement. This event will review C-9B emergency procedures and fulfills the requirement of quarterly emergency procedures simulator training per NAVMC 3500.14. This event can be accomplished as a combined event in the simulator or in the actual aircraft while airborne or sitting on the deck.

Performance Standard. Comply with C-9B NFM emergency procedures.

3.21.2   NATOPS Evaluations (NTPS)

3.21.2.1 Purpose. Provide annual NATOPS and CRM evaluation flights.

NTPS-6100   2.0   365   B,R,M   (N*)   E   A   1 C-9B

> Goal. Conduct annual NATOPS evaluation after initial designation (DESG-6200).
>
> Requirement. Proficiency in the utilization of all aspects of the C-9B. The proficiency expected by the evaluator in this flight shall be commensurate with the experience of the Crew Chief under evaluation.
>
> Performance Standard. The performance expected by the evaluator in this flight shall be commensurate with the experience level of the Crew Chief under evaluation.
>
> Prerequisite. ACAD-6000, ACAD-6001

NTPS-6101   2.0   365   B,R,M   (N*)   E   A   1 C-9B

> Goal. Conduct annual CRM evaluation.
>
> Requirement. Perform initial/annual CRM flight evaluation per applicable directives. May be flown in conjunction with annual NATOPS evaluation flight or initial designation flight (DESG-6200).
>
> Performance Standard. Performance standards will be according to the C-9B NFM.
>
> Prerequisite. ACAD-6005

3.21.3   Designation Flights (DESG)

3.21.3.1 Purpose. To provide an evaluation flight for designation as a Crew Chief upon completion of either the basic or refresher POI.

3.21.3.2 General. CCUI will successfully complete a flight evaluation administered by a designated CCE/CCI.

DESG-6200   3.0   *   B,R   (N*)   E   A   1 C-9B

> Goal. CCUI evaluation flight. CCUI to demonstrate the ability to meet NATOPS qualification per Chapter 18 NATOPS evaluation criteria. The flight evaluation is designed to measure with maximum objectivity the degree of standardization demonstrated by the CCUI and to ensure safety of flight.
>
> Requirement
>
> > Brief/Discuss
> >
> > > The CCUI should be prepared to brief/discuss all previously introduced material.
> >
> > Review/Evaluate
> >
> > > All previously introduced training shall be covered with particular attention given to NATOPS and emergency procedures.
>
> Performance Standard. The CCUI Check should emphasize only those areas that are germane to the Crew Chief duties and demonstrated performance required to safely execute these duties.
>
> Prerequisite. RFAM-2205, IFAM-2301, ACAD-6000, ACAD-6001

3.22   T&R ATTAIN AND MAINTAIN SYLLABUS MATRICES

VMR-1 C-9B
CREW CHIEF

CORE/MISSION/CORE PLUS ATTAIN & MAINTAIN MATRIX

CORE SKILLS INTRODUCTION (1000 PHASE)

T&R DESCRIPTION	STAGE	CODE	RE FLY	ATTAIN PROFICIENCY BASIC POI STAGE	BASIC POI CODE	REFRESHER POI STAGE	REFRESHER POI CODE	MAINTAIN POI STAGE	MAINTAIN POI CODE	PREREQUISITES	CHAINING
Per current contract	SIM	1100	*	SIM	1100	SIM		SIM		1100	
Per current contract	SIM	1101	*		1101					1101	
Per current contract	SIM	1102	*		1102					1102	
Per current contract	SIM	1103	*		1103					1103	
Per current contract	SIM	1104	*		1104					1104	
Per current contract	SIM	1105	*		1105					1105	
Per current contract	SIM	1106	*		1106					1106	
Per current contract	SIM	1107	*		1107					1107	
Per current contract	SIM	1108	*		1108					1108	
Per current contract	SIM	1109	*		1109					1109	
Per current contract	SIM	1110	*		1110					1110	
Per current contract	SIM	1111	*		1111						
APU/Servicing	FAM	1300	*	FAM	1300	FAM		FAM		1300	
Emergency Procedures	FAM	1301	*		1301					1301	
AC/DC Power, and Fuel	FAM	1302	*		1302					1302	
Hyd and Landing Gear	FAM	1303	*		1303					1303	
Flt Controls and pneu	FAM	1304	*		1304					1304	
Fire and Oxygen	FAM	1305	*		1305					1305	
Progress Check	FAM	1306	*		1306		1306				

CORE SKILLS (2000 PHASE)

T&R DESCRIPTION	STAGE	CODE	RE FLY	ATTAIN PROFICIENCY BASIC POI STAGE	BASIC POI CODE	REFRESHER POI STAGE	REFRESHER POI CODE	MAINTAIN POI STAGE	MAINTAIN POI CODE	PREREQUISITES	CHAINING
Per current contract	RECSIM	S2100R	730	RECSIM	S2100R	RECSIM	S2100R	RECSIM	S2100R	None	
Per current contract	RECSIM	S2101R	730		S2101R		S2101R		S2101R	2100	
Per current contract	RECSIM	S2102R	730		S2102R		S2102R		S2102R	2101	
Night EP Rev	RFAM	2200	*	RFAM	2100	RFAM		RFAM		1306	
Night Rev, AC/DC,	RFAM	2201	*		2101					2200	
Landing Gear, Flight	RFAM	2202	*		2102					1306	
Pneumatic, Fire & Oxy	RFAM	2203	*		2103					2202	
Progress Check	RFAM	2204R	*		2104R		2204R			2203, 2201	
1000/2000 Series Rev	RFAM	2205R	90		2105R		2205R		2205R	2204	
International FAM	IFAM	2301R	365	IFAM	2301R	IFAM	2301R	IFAM	2301R	1306	3100,3200,2205

MISSION SKILLS (3000 PHASE)

T&R DESCRIPTION	STAGE	CODE	RE FLY	ATTAIN PROFICIENCY BASIC POI STAGE	BASIC POI CODE	REFRESHER POI STAGE	REFRESHER POI CODE	MAINTAIN POI STAGE	MAINTAIN POI CODE	PREREQUISITES	CHAINING
Passenger Mission	OSA	3100R	180	OSA	3100R	OSA	3100R	OSA	3100R	1306	3200,2205
Cargo Mission	ALS	3200R	180	ALS	3200R	ALS	3200R	ALS	3200R	1306	3100,2205

NAVMC 3500.31A
22 Nov 11

3.23   T&R SYLLABUS MATRIX

VMR-1 CREW CHIEF T&R MATRIX

STAGE	TRNG CODE	T&R DESCRIPTION	POI	E	DEVICE	# OF A/C	CON	RE FLY	# OF ACAD	ACAD TIME	# OF SIM	SIM TIME	# OF FLTS	FLT TIME	PREREQUISITE	NOTES	CHAINING	EVENT CONV
		CORE SKILL INTRODUCTION TRAINING (1000 PHASE EVENTS)																
		SIMULATOR (SIM)																
SIM	1100	Per current contract	B		FBS		(N*)	*				4.0						N/A
SIM	1101	Per current contract	B		FBS		(N*)	*				4.0			1100			N/A
SIM	1102	Per current contract	B		FBS		(N*)	*				4.0			1101			N/A
SIM	1103	Per current contract	B		FBS		(N*)	*				4.0			1102			N/A
SIM	1104	Per current contract	B		S		(N*)	*				4.0			1103			N/A
SIM	1105	Per current contract	B		S		(N*)	*				4.0			1104			N/A
SIM	1106	Per current contract	B		S		(N*)	*				4.0			1105			N/A
SIM	1107	Per current contract	B		S		(N*)	*				4.0			1106			N/A
SIM	1108	Per current contract	B		S		(N*)	*				4.0			1107			N/A
SIM	1109	Per current contract	B		S		(N*)	*				4.0			1108			N/A
SIM	1110	Per current contract	B		S		(N*)	*				4.0			1109			N/A
SIM	1111	Per current contract	B		S		(N*)	*				4.0			1110			N/A
		TOTAL SIM STAGE							0	0.0	12	48.0	0	0.0				
		FAMILIARIZATION (FAM)																
FAM	1300	APU/Servicing	B		A		(N*)	*						3.0	Designated 2LM			100
FAM	1301	Emergency Procedures	B		A		(N*)	*						3.0	1300			110
FAM	1302	AC/DC Power, and Fuel	B		A		(N*)	*						3.0	1301			120
FAM	1303	Hydraulics and Landing Gear	B		A		(N*)	*						3.0	1302			130
FAM	1304	Flight Controls and Pneumatics	B		A		(N*)	*						3.0	1303			140
FAM	1305	Fire Warning/Protection and Oxygen	B		A		(N*)	*						3.0	1304			150
FAM	1306	Progress Check	B,R	E	A		(N*)	*						3.0	1305			160
		TOTAL FAM STAGE							0	0.0			7	21.0				
		TOTAL CORE SKILL INTRODUCTION PHASE (1000 PHASE)							0	0.0	12	48.0	7	21.0				
		CORE SKILL TRAINING (2000 PHASE EVENTS)																
		RECURRENT SIMULATORS (RECSIM)																
RECSIM	2100	Refresher 1	B,R,M		S		(N*)	730				4.0						N/A
RECSIM	2101	Refresher 2	B,R,M		S		(N*)	730				4.0			2100			N/A

3-24

Enclosure (1)

VMR-1 CREW CHIEF T&R MATRIX

STAGE	TRNG CODE	T&R DESCRIPTION	POI	DEVICE E	DEVICE S	# OF A/C	CON	RE FLY	# OF ACAD	ACAD TIME	# OF SIM	SIM TIME	# OF FLTS	FLT TIME	PREREQUISITE	NOTES	CHAINING	EVENT CONV
RECSIM	2102	Refresher 3	B,R,M		S		(N*)	730			3	4.0			2101			N/A
		TOTAL RECURRENT STAGE							0	0.0	3	12.0	0	0.0				
		REVIEW FAMILIARIZATION FLIGHTS (RFAM)																
RFAM	2200	Night Introduction /Emergency Procedures Review	B		A	1	N*	*						5.0				200
RFAM	2201	Night Review, AC/DC, Fuel, Hydraulics Review	B		A	1	N*	*						5.0				210
RFAM	2202	Landing Gear, Flight Controls Review	B		A	1	(N*)	*						5.0				220
RFAM	2203	Pneumatic, Fire Warning/ Protection and Oxygen Systems Review	B		A	1	(N*)	*						5.0				230
RFAM	2204	Progress Check	B,R	E	A	1	(N*)	*						5.0				240
RFAM	2205	1000/2000 Series Review	B,R,M		A	1	(N*)	90						4.0				310
		TOTAL RFAM STAGE							0	0.0	0	0.0	6	29.0				
		INTERNATIONAL/TRANS OCEANIC (IFAM)																
IFAM	2301	International/Trans Oceanic Review	B,R,M		A	1	(N*)	365					1	5.0			3100,3200,2205	320
		TOTAL IFAM STAGE							0	0.0	0	0.0	1	5.0				
		TOTAL CORE SKILL PHASE (2000 PHASE)							3	12.0	7	34.0						
		MISSION SKILL TRAINING (3000 PHASE)																
		OPERATIONAL SUPPORT AIRLIFT (OSA)																
OSA	3100	Passenger Mission	B,R,M		A	1	(N*)	180					1	5.0	1306		3200,2205	N/A
		TOTAL OSA STAGE							0	0.0	0	0.0	1	5.0				
		AIR LOGISTICS SUPPORT (ALS)																
ALS	3200	Cargo Mission	B,R,M		A	1	(N*)	180					1	5.0	1306		3100,2205	N/A
		TOTAL ALS STAGE							0	0.0	0	0.0	1	5.0				
		TOTAL MISSION SKILL PHASE (3000 PHASE)							0	0.0	0	0.0	2	10.0				
		TOTAL 1000, 2000, & 3000 PHASE							15	60.0	16	65.0						

Enclosure (1)

VMR-1 CREW CHIEF T&R MATRIX

STAGE	TRNG CODE	T&R DESCRIPTION	POI	DEVICE E	DEVICE A	# OF A/C	CON	RE FLY	# OF ACAD	ACAD TIME	# OF SIM	SIM TIME	# OF FLTS	FLT TIME	PREREQUISITE	NOTES	CHAINING	EVENT CONV
														INSTRUCTOR TRAINING (5000 PHASE EVENTS)			
												INSTRUCTOR UNDER TRAINING (IUT)					
IUT	5100	Instructor Intro	B		A	1	(N*)	*						3.0	6200		2205	500
IUT	5101	Instructor Eval	B	E	A	1	(N*)	*						3.0	5100		2205	501
IUT	5102	NATOPS Evaluator Flight	B,R,M		A	1	(N*)	*					3	3.0	5101		2205	601
		TOTAL IUT STAGE							0	0.0	0	0.0	3	9.0				
	INSTRUCTOR TRAINING (5000 PHASE EVENTS) TOTAL								0	0.0	0	0.0	3	9.0				
		REQUIREMENT, QUALIFICATIONS, AND DESIGNATIONS (RQD) (6000 PHASE)																
									RQD ACADEMICS (ACAD)								
ACAD	6000	NATOPS Open Exam	B,R,M	E				365		4.0							N/A	N/A
ACAD	6001	NATOPS Closed Exam	B,R,M	E				365		2.0					6000			N/A
ACAD	6002	NATOPS Oral Exam	B,R,M	E				365		2.0					6000,6001			N/A
ACAD	6005	CRM Ground Class	B,R,M	E				365		2.0								N/A
ACAD	6006	Monthly EP Exam	B,R,M	E				30		1.0								N/A
ACAD	6007	90 EP Practical Review	B,R,M		S/A	1		90		1.0								N/A
		TOTAL ACAD STAGE							0	12.0	0	0.0	0	0.0				
									NATOPS								
NTPS	6100	NATOPS Evaluation	B,R,M	E	A	1	(N*)	365					1	2.0	6000,6001		2205	600
NTPS	6101	CRM Flight Evaluation	B,R,M	E	A	1	(N*)	365					1	2.0	6005			N/A
		NATOPS TOTAL							0	0.0	0	0.0	2	4.0				
									CC DESIGNATIONS (DESG)								
DESG	6200	CC Designation Flight	B,R	E	A	1	(N*)	365					1	3.0			2205	390
		TOTAL DESG STAGE							0	0.0	0	0.0	1	3.0				
		RQD TOTAL (6000 PHASE)							6	12.0	0	0.0	3	7.0				
		TOTAL 5000,6000 STAGES							6	12.0	0	0.0	6	16.0				
		TOTAL 1000,2000,3000,5000,6000 STAGES							6	12.0	15	72.0	22	81.0				

CHAPTER 4

2ND LOADMASTER

4.0   INDIVIDUAL TRAINING AND READINESS REQUIREMENTS. This T&R syllabus is based on specific goals and performance standards designed to ensure individual proficiency in Core, Mission, and Core Plus Skills. The goal of this chapter is to develop individual and unit war fighting capabilities.

4.1   TRAINING PROGRESSION MODEL. This model represents the recommended training progression for the average C-9B 2nd Loadmaster (2LM). Units should use the model as a guide to generate individual training plans.

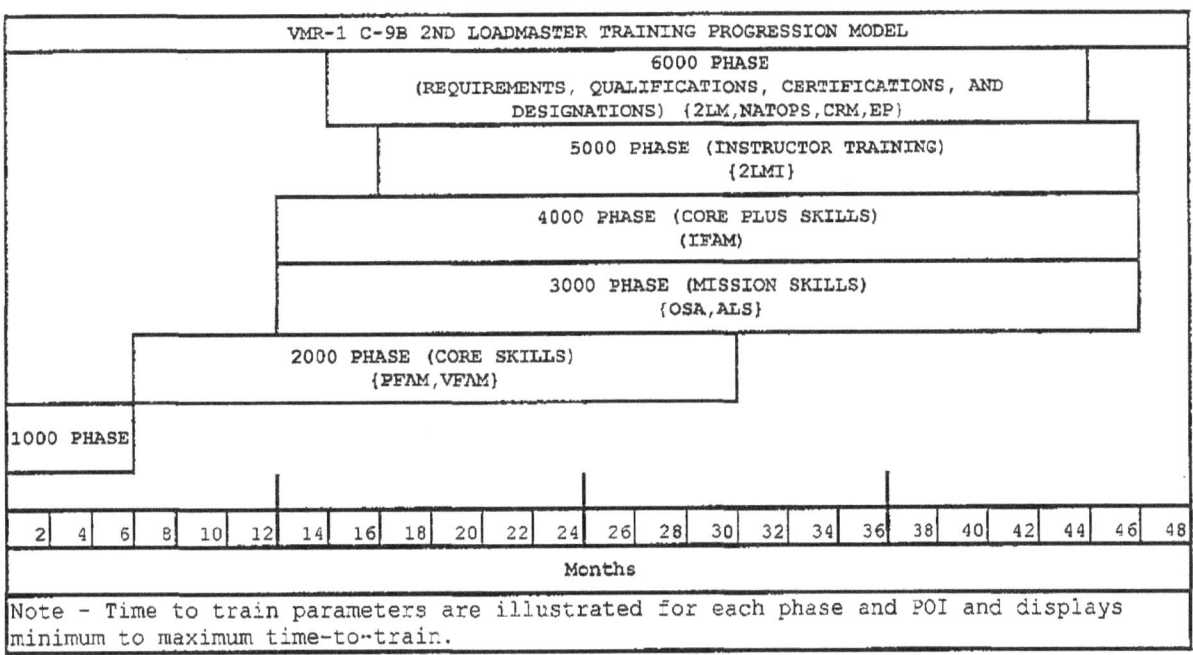

Note - Time to train parameters are illustrated for each phase and POI and displays minimum to maximum time-to-train.

4.2   ABBREVIATIONS

VMR-1 C-9B 2ND LOADMASTER	
CORE/MISSION/CORE PLUS SKILL ABBREVIATIONS	
CORE SKILLS (2000 Phase)	
FAM	Familiarization
PFAM	Passenger Familiarization
VFAM	VIP Familiarization
MISSION SKILLS (3000 Phase)	
OSA	Operational Support Airlift
ALS	Air Logistics Support
CORE PLUS SKILLS (4000 Phase)	
IFAM	International/Transoceanic Familiarization
INSTRUCTOR (5000 Phase)	
2LMI	Second Loadmaster Instructor
QUALIFICATIONS AND DESIGNATIONS (6000 Phase)	
ACAD	Academics
NTPS	NATOPS
2LM	Second Loadmaster
EP	Emergency Procedures

4.3   DEFINITIONS

TERM	DEFINITION
Core Model	The Core Model is the basic foundation or standardized format by which all T&Rs are constructed. The Core Model provides the capability of quantifying both unit and individual training requirements and measuring readiness. This is accomplished by linking community Mission Statements, Mission Essential Task Lists, Output Standards, Core Skill Proficiency Requirements and Combat Leadership Matrices
Core Skill	Fundamental, environmental, or conditional capabilities required to perform basic functions. These basic functions serve as tactical enablers that allow crews to progress to the more complex Mission Skills. Primarily 2000 Phase events but may be introduced in the 1000 Phase.
Mission Skill	Mission Skills enable a unit to execute a specific MET. They are comprised of advanced event(s) that are focused on MET performance and draw upon the knowledge, aeronautical abilities, and situational awareness developed during Core Skill training. 3000 Phase events.
Core Plus Skill	Training events that can be theater specific or that have a low likelihood of occurrence. They may be Fundamental, environmental, or conditional capabilities required to perform basic functions. 4000 Phase events.
Core Plus Mission	Training events that can be theater specific or that have a low likelihood of occurrence. They are comprised of advanced event(s) that are focused on Core Plus MET performance and draw upon the knowledge, aeronautical abilities, and situational awareness. 4000 Phase events.
Core Skill Proficiency (CSP)	CSP is a measure of training completion for 2000 Phase events. CSP is attained by executing all events listed in the Attain Table for each Core Skill. The individual must be simultaneously proficient in all events within that Core Skill to attain CSP.
Mission Skill Proficiency (MSP)	MSP is a measure of training completion for 3000 Phase events. MSP is attained by executing all events listed in the Attain Table for each Mission Skill. The individual must be simultaneously proficient in all events within that Mission Skill to attain MSP. MSP is directly related to Training Readiness.
Core Plus Skill Proficiency (CPSP)	CPSP is a measure of training completion for 4000 Phase "Skill" events. CPSP is attained by executing all events listed in the Attain Table for each Core Plus Skill. The individual must be simultaneously proficient in all events within that Core Plus Skill to attain CPSP
Core Plus Mission Proficiency (CPMP)	CPMP is a measure of training completion for 4000 Phase "Mission" events. CPMP is attained by executing all events listed in the Attain Table for each Core Plus Mission. The individual must be simultaneously proficient in all events within that Core Plus Mission to attain CPMP

4.4   INDIVIDUAL CORE/MISSION/CORE PLUS SKILL PROFICIENCY REQUIREMENTS

4.4.1   Management of individual CSP/MSP/CPSP/CPMP serves as the foundation for developing proficiency requirements in DRRS.

4.4.2   Individual CSP is a "Yes/No" status assigned to an individual by Core Skill. When an individual attains and maintains CSP in a Core Skill, the individual counts towards CMMR Unit CSP requirements for that Core Skill.

4.4.3   Proficiency is attained by individual Core/Mission/Core Plus Skill and the training events to be executed within that skill set are determined by POI assignment (Basic, Transition, Conversion, Series Conversion, or Refresher).

4.4.4   Once proficiency has been attained by Core/Mission/Core Plus Skill (by any POI assignment) then the individual maintains proficiency by executing those events within the maintain column. An individual maintains proficiency by individual Core/Mission/Core Plus Skill.

Note
Individuals may be attaining proficiency
in some Core/Mission/Core Plus Skills
while maintaining proficiency in other
Core/Mission/Core Plus Skills.

4.4.5   Once proficiency has been attained, should one lose proficiency in an event in the maintain column, proficiency can be attained by demonstrating proficiency in the event which was delinquent. Should an individual lose proficiency in all events in the Maintain column by Core/Mission/Core Plus Skill, the individual will be assigned to the Refresher POI for that Core/Mission/Core Plus Skill. To regain proficiency for that Core/Mission/Core Plus Skill the individual must demonstrate proficiency in all R-coded events for that Core/Mission/Core Plus Skill.

VMR-1 C-9B 2ND LOADMASTER					
ATTAIN AND MAINTAIN CORE/MISSION/CORE PLUS PROFICIENCY MATRIX BY POI					
ATTAIN PROFICIENCY				MAINTAIN PROFICIENCY	
BASIC POI		REFRESHER POI		MAINTAIN POI	
CORE SKILL (2000 Phase)					
PFAM	2100	PFAM		PFAM	
	2101R		2101R		2101R
VFAM	2200	VFAM		VFAM	
	2201R		2201R		2201R
MISSION SKILL (3000 Phase)					
OSA	3100R	OSA	3100R	OSA	3100R
ALS	3200R	ALS	3200R	ALS	3200R
CORE PLUS SKILL (4000 Phase)					
IFAM	4000	IFAM		IFAM	
	4001R		4001R		4001R
S prefix and blue font = flown in simulator					
R suffix and Grey highlight = R-coded "Refresher" event					

4.5   CERTIFICATION, QUALIFICATION AND DESIGNATION TABLES. The tables below delineate T&R events required to be completed to attain proficiency, initial qualifications and designations. In addition to event requirements, all required stage lectures, briefs, squadron training, prerequisites, and other criteria shall be completed prior to completing final events. Certification, qualification and designation letters signed by the Commanding Officer shall be placed in Aircrew Performance Records (APR) and NATOPS. Loss of proficiency in all qualification events causes the associated qualification to be lost. Regaining a qualification requires completing all R-coded syllabus events associated with that qualification.

4.5.1   INSTRUCTOR DESIGNATIONS

VMR-1 C-9B 2ND LOADMASTER INSTRUCTOR DESIGNATIONS (5000 Phase)	
INSTRUCTOR DESIGNATION	EVENTS
2LM ASSISTANT NATOPS INSTRUCTOR (2LM ANI)	5100,5101
2LM NATOPS EVALUATOR/INSTRUCTOR (2LM NE/NI)	5100,5101,5102

4.5.2   REQUIREMENTS, CERTIFICATIONS, QUALIFICATIONS, AND DESIGNATIONS

4.5.2.1 The tables below delineate T&R events required to be completed to attain initial qualifications and designations. All stage lectures, briefs, squadron training, prerequisites, and open and closed book NATOPS exams shall be complete and graded prior to completing evaluation flights. Qualification and designation letters signed by the Commanding Officer shall be placed in individual NATOPS and APR jackets.

VMR-1 C-9B 2ND LOADMASTER REQUIREMENTS, CERTIFICATIONS, QUALIFICATIONS, AND DESIGNATIONS (R,C,Q,& D) [6000 Phase]	
R,C,Q,& D	EVENTS
QUALIFICATIONS	
NATOPS	6000,6001,6002,6100
CRM	6005,6101
DESIGNATIONS	
2LM	6100,6200

4.6   VMR-1 C-9B 2ND LOADMASTER PROGRAMS OF INSTRUCTION (POI). These tables reflect average time-to-train versus the minimum to maximum time-to-train parameters in the Training Progression Model.

4.6.1   2LM training and designation sets the foundation for follow-on training as a Loadmaster or Crew Chief. Designation as a 2LM is a requirement for a C-9B air crewman to be considered by the squadron Standardization Board for assignment to either the Loadmaster syllabus or Crew Chief syllabus.

4.6.2   Basic POI. A Basic 2nd Loadmaster (2LM) shall be defined as an individual who has no previous experience as a 2LM. The 2LM Under Instruction (2LMUI) shall be screened by the squadron Aircrew Screening Board and approved by the Commanding Officer prior to commencing this POI. Every effort should be made to conduct VIP training codes aboard actual VIP missions, however, it is permissible to conduct simulated VIP missions as required in order to continue the student through the syllabus. All decisions as to POI eligibility rest with the Commanding Officer. The 2LM Under Instruction shall be considered qualified to function as a qualified 2LM on both CONUS and OCONUS missions upon completion of the 2LM designation flight (DESG-6200). Upon completion of the 2LM designation, the 2LM must complete OSA-3100 and ALS-3200 under the supervision of an instructor prior to performing those duties individually. Additionally, the 2LM becomes eligible for consideration by the squadron Standardization Board for assignment to the Loadmaster or Crew Chief syllabus upon designation as a 2LM. The International/Trans Oceanic flights (IFAM 4000 and IFAM 4001) are established to ensure the 2LM has been exposed to Overwater/International procedures prior to assignment to the 2LM NATOPS Instructor/Evaluator Phases. As such, these flights shall be complete prior to commencing the 2LM Instructor or 2LM NATOPS Instructor/Evaluator syllabus.

VMR-1 C-9B 2ND LOADMASTER Basic POI		
Weeks	Phase of Instruction	Unit
1	Water Survival/Flight Physiology	NAWSTP
1	Ground Training	VMR-1
3	Core Skill Introduction (1000 Phase)	VMR-1
3	Core Skill (2000 Phase)	VMR-1
3	Mission Skill (3000 Phase)	VMR-1

4.6.3   Refresher POI. The 2LMUI must have flown in the capacity as a C-9B 2LM during the previous two years in order to be eligible for this refresher POI. The 2LMUI shall have been recommended by the squadron Standardization Board and approved by the Commanding Officer prior to commencing this refresher POI. All decisions as to POI eligibility rest with the Commanding Officer.

4.6.3.1 A 2LM who has been assigned to other duty preventing currency in the C-9B aircraft for a period exceeding 24 months is not eligible for Refresher

2LM training and must complete the basic POI prior to re-designation as a 2LM.

	VMR-1 C-9B 2ND LOADMASTER Refresher POI		
Weeks	Phase of Instruction	Unit
1	Water Survival/Flight Physiology *	NAWSTP
2	Core Introduction (1000 Phase)	VMR-1
2	Core Skill (2000 Phase)	VMR-1
2	Mission Skill (3000 Phase)	VMR-1
* Required only if NAWSTP Swim Qualification is expired.		

4.6.4   POI FOR INSTRUCTOR 2ND LOADMASTER UNDER TRAINING (IUT). The 2LMIUT shall have been recommended by the squadron Standardization Board and approved by the Commanding Officer prior to commencing this POI. All decisions as to POI eligibility rest with the Commanding Officer. The 2LMIUT will complete IFAM-4000 and IFAM-4001 prior to assignment to the 2LM Instructor or 2LM NATOPS Instructor/Evaluator Training.

	VMR-1 C-9B 2ND LOADMASTER Instructor POI		
Weeks	Phase of Instruction	Unit
1	2LM Instructor Training	VMR-1
1	2LM NATOPS Evaluator Training	VMR-1

4.7   SYLLABUS NOTES

4.7.1   Environmental Conditions Matrix

	Environmental Conditions	
Code	Meaning
D	Shall be flown during hours of daylight: (by exception - there is no use of a symbol)
N*	Shall be flown during hours of darkness must be flown unaided
(N*)	May be flown during hours of darkness - If flown during hours of darkness must be flown unaided
Note - If the event is to be flown in the simulator the Simulator Instructor shall set the desired environmental conditions for the event.	

4.7.2   Device Matrix

	DEVICE (Aviation Flying)	
Symbol	Meaning
A	Flown in aircraft
A/S	Aircraft preferred may be flown in simulator
S	Flown in simulator
S/A	Simulator preferred may be flown in aircraft
Note - If the event is to be flown in the simulator the Simulator Instructor shall set the desired environmental conditions for the event.	

4.7.3   Program of Instruction Matrix

	PROGRAM OF INSTRUCTION MATRIX		
Program of Instruction (POI)	Symbol	Aviation Flying	Aviation Ground
Basic	B	Initial MOS/Skill Training	Initial MOS training
Refresher	R	DIFDEN to DIFOPS in same T/M/S	Return to community from non (MOS/Skill) associated tour
Maintain	M	All individuals who have attained CSP/MSP/CPP by initial POI assignment are re-assigned to the M POI to maintain proficiency.	
*Many communities will assign transition and conversion aircrew to the basic POI.			

4.7.4   Event Terms

EVENT TERMS	
TERM	**DESCRIPTION**
Discuss	An explanation of systems, procedures, or maneuvers during the brief, in flight, or post flight. Student is responsible for knowledge of procedures.
Demonstrate	The description and performance of a particular maneuver/event by the instructor, observed by the 2LMUI/student. The 2LMUI/student is responsible for knowledge of the procedures prior to the demonstration of a required maneuver/student.
Introduce	The instructor may demonstrate a procedure or maneuver to a student, or may coach the 2LMUI through the maneuver without demonstration. The 2LMUI performs the procedures or maneuver with coaching as necessary. The 2LMUI is responsible for knowledge of the procedures.
Practice	The performance of a maneuver or procedure by the 2LMUI/student that may have been previously introduced in order to attain a specified level of performance.
Review	Demonstrated proficiency of a maneuver by the 2LMUI/student.
Evaluate	Any flight designed to evaluate aircrew standardization that does not fit another category such as SARCK, HACCK, T2PCK, etc.
E-Coded	This term means that documentation (ATF) is required each time the event is logged. Requires evaluation by a certified standardization instructor (NATOPS I, WTI, INST Evaluator etc.)

4.8   CORE SKILL INTRODUCTION FRS ACADEMIC PHASE (0000 Phase). There are no 0000 phase events in the C-9B T&R manual. However, the squadron training listed below is required.

4.8.1   The following one-week ground training syllabus is intended as squadron-level training for 2nd Loadmasters during initial qualification. Refresher 2nd Loadmasters are exempt from this ground training syllabus. This ground training may be conducted concurrently with the flight training syllabus. However, the ground training syllabus must be complete prior to the designation flight (DESG-6200).

General aircraft description
Aircraft systems
Aircraft emergency equipment and systems
Emergency procedures
2LM procedures and responsibilities
Personal fying equipment requirements
Aircraft mission
NATOPS open and closed book examinations

4.9   CORE SKILL INTRODUCTION PHASE (1000). The core skill introduction phase is designed to familiarize the 2LMUI with C-9B ground servicing, normal procedures, CRM, systems operation and limitations, and emergency procedures.

4.10   CORE SKILL INTRODUCTION STAGES (1000)

PARAGRAPH	STAGE
4.10.1	Familiarization (FAM)

4.10.1   Familiarization Flights (FAM)

4.10.1.1   Purpose. Familiarize the 2LMUI with the C-9B aircraft. Introduce NATOPS procedures, operation and servicing of aircraft equipment, and all duties and procedures required of a qualified 2LM.

4.10.1.2   Crew Requirements. TAC, T2P, CC, LM, 2LMI, 2LMUI

FAM-1300   2.0   *   B   (N*)   A   1 C-9B

    Goal. Cabin facilities introduction.

    Requirement

        Discuss/Demonstrate/Introduce

            Preflight responsibilities
            Operation of the heads
            Coffee makers
            Freezer
            Refrigerator and ovens
            Duties of the 2LM during the flight
            Post flight duties

        Review

            Ground training material

    Performance Standard. Student will have a general understanding of the responsibilities of a 2LM.

    Prerequisite. Nomination by Aircrew Screening Board, approval of Commanding Officer, successful completion of water survival and flight physiology.

FAM-1301   2.0   *   B   (N*)   A   1 C-9B

    Goal. Servicing introduction and review of previous instruction.

    Requirement

        Discuss/Demonstrate/Introduce

            Servicing of heads
            Maintenance of servicing carts
            Review of holding tank capabilities
            Servicing of fresh water cart
            Capacities of the holding tank

        Review

            Previously covered material

    Performance Standard. 2LMUI will demonstrate proficiency in all previously covered training and have a general knowledge of all items covered pertaining to FAM-1300.

    Prerequisite. FAM-1300

FAM-1302   2.0   *   B,R   (N*)   A   1 C-9B

    Goal. Introduce the 2LM responses/actions required during each ground and airborne emergency.

    Requirement

        Discuss/Demonstrate/Introduce

            Rapid depressurization/emergency descent
            Fuselage fire
            Cabin smoke/fume elimination
            In-flight hazardous spill
            Crash landing/abnormal landing/ditching
            Refilling of walk around oxygen bottles
            Location and use of all emergency equipment

        Review

             Previously covered material

    Performance Standard. 2LMUI will demonstrate proficiency regarding all previous training and be introduced to new material. Student should be able to demonstrate all asterisk emergency procedure items which involve the 2LM position.

Prerequisite. FAM-1301

4.11   CORE SKILL PHASE (2000)

4.11.1   General

Core Skill Phase in the C-9B introduces the 2LMUI to the requirements and responsibilities when carrying passengers, cargo, and VIPs (Code 7 and higher).

4.12   CORE SKILL INTRODUCTION STAGES (2000)

PARAGRAPH	STAGE
4.12.1	Passenger Familiarization (PFAM)
4.12.2	VIP Familiarization (VFAM)

4.12.1   Passenger Familiarization (PFAM)

4.12.1.1 Purpose. Instruct the 2LMUI in proper procedures for passenger handling.

4.12.1.2 Crew Requirements. TAC, T2P, LM, 2LMI, 2LMUI

PFAM-2100   2.0   *   B   (N*)   A   1 C-9B

Goal. 2LMUI will be instructed on 2LM responsibilities on a passenger flight.

Requirement

Discuss

Passenger and baggage handling
Responsibilities on turn-around
Handling, storing, preparing, and serving in-flight meals
RON procedures

Demonstrate/Introduce

Passenger and baggage handling
Responsibilities on turn-around
Handling, storing, preparing, and serving in-flight meals
RON procedures

Review

Previously covered material as necessary

Performance Standard. Student will demonstrate proficiency in all previously covered training and have a general knowledge of all items covered pertaining to FAM-1301.

Prerequisite. FAM-1302

PFAM-2101   2.0   365   B,R,M   (N*)   A   1 C-9B

Goal. 2LMUI will demonstrate proficiency in all aspects of duties and responsibilities on a passenger flight.

Requirement

Discuss

Passenger and baggage handling
Responsibilities on turn-around

Handling, storing, preparing, and serving in-flight meals
RON procedures

Review

Passenger and baggage handling
Responsibilities on turn-around
Handling, storing, preparing, and serving in-flight meals
RON procedures
Previously covered material as necessary

Performance Standard. 2LMUI will demonstrate proficiency in all previously covered training and have a general knowledge of all items covered pertaining to FAM-2101.

Prerequisite. PFAM-2100

4.12.2 VIP Familiarization (VFAM)

4.12.2.1 Purpose. Instruct the 2LMUI in the proper procedures when carrying a VIP passenger.

4.12.2.2 Crew Requirements. TAC, T2P, LM, 2LMI, 2LMUI

VFAM-2200   2.0   ^   B   (N*)   A   1 C-9B

Goal. 2LMUI will be instructed on responsibilities on a VIP flight.

Requirement

Discuss
Unique procedures during the flight
Uniform and appearance during the flight

Demonstrate/Introduce
Unique procedures during the flight
Uniform and appearance during the flight

Review
Previously covered material as necessary

Performance Standard. Student will demonstrate proficiency in all previously covered training and have a general knowledge of all items covered pertaining to VFAM-2200.

Prerequisite. FAM-1302

VFAM-2201   2.0   365   B,R,M   (N*)   A   1 C-9B

Goal. 2LMUI will demonstrate proficiency in all aspects of duties and responsibilities on a VIP flight.

Requirement

Discuss
Unique procedures during the flight
Uniform and appearance during the flight

Review
Unique procedures during the flight
Uniform and appearance during the flight
Previously covered material as necessary

Performance Standard. 2LMUI will demonstrate proficiency in all previously covered training and conduct VIP procedures with minimal supervision from the 2LM instructor.

Prerequisite. VFAM-2200

4.13   MISSION SKILLS PHASE (3000)

4.13.1   General. The Mission Skill Phase is designed to familiarize the 2LMUI with the unique missions and challenges associated with the VMR-1, C-9B. Mission Skills are designed to fulfill the requirements of the C-9B Mission Essential Task List as defined by the associated Marine Corps Task (MCT).

4.14   MISSION SKILL STAGES (3000)

PARAGRAPH	STAGE
4.14.1	Operational Support Airlift (OSA)
4.14.2	Air Logistics Support (ALS)

4.14.1   Operational Support Airlift (OSA)

4.14.1.1 Purpose. This event is designed to fulfill the requirement set in MCT 1.3.4.1.2, conduct OSA.

4.14.1.2 General. It is understood that many missions will be a combination of both passenger and cargo transportation and both codes will be used when filling out the NAVFLIR. Both codes are made available for flights that clearly fall into a single category.

4.14.1.3 Crew Requirement. Full mission crew.

OSA-3100   2.0   180   B,R,M   (N*)   A   1   C-9B
    Goal. Introduce the 2LMUI to the JOSAC/ASM passenger mission or provide continued update to the skills of the 2LM while performing the passenger mission.
    Requirement. 2LM/2LMUI will execute a JOSAC/ASM passenger mission and perform all 2LM flight related duties safely and proficiently.
    Performance Standard. 2LM/2LMUI will safely conduct all duties related to the JOSAC passenger mission with proficiency.
    Prerequisite. DESG-6200

4.14.2   Air Logistics Support (ALS)

4.14.2.1 Purpose. This event is designed to fulfill the requirement set in MMC 4.3.8, conduct ALS.

4.14.2.2 General. It is understood that many missions will be a combination of both passenger and cargo transportation and both codes will be used when filling out the NAVFLIR. Both codes are made available for flights that clearly fall into a single category.

4.14.2.3 Crew Requirement. Full mission crew.

ALS-3200   2.0   180   B,R,M   (N*)   A   1   C-9B
    Goal. Introduce the 2LMUI to the C-9B cargo mission or provide continued update to the 2LM skills used while performing the cargo missions.
    Requirement. 2LM/2LMUI will execute a JOSAC cargo mission and perform all 2LM flight related duties safely and proficiently.
    Performance Standard. 2LM/2LMUI will safely conduct all duties related to the JOSAC cargo mission with proficiency
    Prerequisite. DESG-6200

4.15   CORE PLUS SKILL PHASE (4000)

4.15.1   General. Core Skill Plus Phase in the C-9B introduces the 2LMUI to the requirements and responsibilities when flying internationally.

4.16   CORE PLUS SKILL STAGES (4000)

PARAGRAPH	STAGE
4.16.1	International/Tansoceanic Familiarization

4.16.1   International/Transoceanic Familiarization (IFAM)

4.16.1.1 Purpose. To instruct the 2LMUI in procedures required when flying on IFAM flights. This phase is established to prepare the 2LMUI for follow-on instruction in the 2LM Instructor and 2LM NATOPS Evaluator Phases.

4.16.1.2 Crew Requirements. TAC, T2P, LM, 2LMI, 2LMUI

IFAM-4000   3.0   *   B   (N*)   A   1 C-9B

    Goal. 2LMUI will be instructed on responsibilities on an International/Transoceanic flight.

    Requirement

        Discuss

            Over water passenger brief
            Location and use of all rafts, slides and life vests
            Ditching procedures
            International procedures

        Demonstrate/Introduce

            Over water passenger brief
            Location and use of all rafts, slides and life vests
            Ditching procedures
            International procedures

        Review

            Previously covered material as necessary

    Performance Standard. 2LMUI will demonstrate proficiency in all previously covered training and have a general knowledge of all items covered pertaining to IFAM-2300.

    Prerequisite. FAM-1302

IFAM-4001   3.0   365   B,R,M   (N*)   A   1 C-9B

    Goal. 2LM/2LMUI will demonstrate proficiency in all aspects of duties and responsibilities on an IFAM flight.

    Requirement

        Discuss

            Over water passenger brief
            Location and use of all rafts, slides and life vests
            Ditching procedures
            International procedures

        Review

            Over water passenger brief
            Location and use of all rafts, slides and life vests
            Ditching procedures

International procedures

Performance Standard. 2LM/2LMUI will demonstrate proficiency in all previously covered training and conduct all overwater related 2LM duties with minimal supervision. Student needs to be capable of independently conducting all 2LM duties related to IFAM flight.

Prerequisite. IFAM-2300

4.17   INSTRUCTOR TRAINING PHASE (5000)

4.17.1   General. The instructor training phase is designed to provide the squadron with a cadre of qualified instructors needed to ensure quality training at all times.

PARAGRAPH	STAGE
4.18.1	Instructor Under Training (IUT)

4.18   Instructor Training Stages (5000)

4.18.1   Instructor Under Training (IUT)

4.18.1.1 Purpose. Develop qualified 2nd Loadmaster instructors with the ability to teach all phases of C-9B flight and mission requirements.

4.18.1.2 General. A 2LMI is qualified to instruct in all phases of aircraft operations. A 2LM must have 100 hours (waiverable by the Commanding Officer) in the C-9B before being recommended for the instructor syllabus.

4.18.1.2 Crew Requirements. TAC, T2P, CC, LM, 2LMI/E, 2LMIUT, 2LM

IUT-5100   3.0   *   B,R   (N*)   E   A   1 C-9B

Goal. Instruction introduction.
Requirement
    Brief/Discuss
        Conduct of training flight
        Instructional techniques
        T&R and syllabus evaluation forms
    Review
        The 2LMI shall observe a 2LMIUT instruct a 2LMUI on a syllabus flight. The 2LMI shall demonstrate emphasis upon evaluating the 2LMIUT's instruction of aircraft servicing, passenger handling, and emergency procedures.
Performance Standard. 2LMIUT should have a solid knowledge of aircraft and 2LM responsibilities during all aspects of ground and flight operations.
Prerequisite. DESG-6200, IFAM-4001, 100 hours in C-9B as a 2LM

IUT-5101   3.0   *   B,R   (N*)   E   A   1 C-9B

Goal. Qualify the 2LM as a 2LM ANI.
Requirement
    Discuss
        Conduct of evaluation flight
        Review all 2LM/2LMI ground and flight responsibilities, publications, and required documentation

Review. The 2LM shall perform all duties of a 2LMI on a flight with a 2LMUI while being evaluated by a 2LM NATOPS Instructor/Evaluator.

Performance Standard. 2LM will demonstrate the requisite maturity, instructional ability, and standardization expected of a 2LMI.

Prerequisite. IUT-5100

IUT-5102   3.0   *   B,R   (N*) E   A   1 C-9B

Goal. Qualify the 2LMI as a NATOPS Instructor/Evaluator 2LM NI/NE.

Requirement

Discuss

Conduct of evaluation flight
Responsibilities of the 2LM NI/NE

Review

The 2LM ANI shall be evaluated by a 2LM NATOPS Evaluator while instructing a 2LMUI
The 2LM ANI being evaluated must display the maturity, integrity, and knowledge of the aircraft required to conduct a NATOPS evaluation

Performance Standard. Student will demonstrate the requisite maturity, instructional ability, and standardization expected of a 2LM NI/NE.

Prerequisite. IUT-5101

4.19   REQUIREMENTS, CERTIFICATIONS, QUALIFICATIONS, AND DESIGNATIONS (RCQD) PHASE (6000)

4.19.1   General. The 6000 phase encompasses the events required to maintain currency with all certifications, qualifications, and designations.

4.20   REQUIREMENTS, CERTIFICATIONS, QUALIFICATIONS, AND DESIGNATIONS (RCQD) STAGES (6000)

PARAGRAPH	STAGE
4.21.1	Academics (ACAD)
4.21.2	NATOPS (NTPS)
4.21.3	Designations (DESG)

4.21.1   Academics (ACAD)

4.21.1.1 Purpose. To complete the academic requirements for subsequent annual evaluation flights.

ACAD-6000   1.0   365   B,R,M   E

Goal. The NATOPS open book examination shall consist of, but not be limited to the question bank. The purpose of the open book examination is to evaluate the 2nd Loadmaster's knowledge of the appropriate publications and the aircraft.

Performance Standard. Achieve a minimum score of 3.5 on the open book examination.

ACAD-6001   1.0   365   B,R,M   E

    Goal. The purpose of the NATOPS closed book examination is to evaluate the 2nd Loadmaster's knowledge of the concerning normal/emergency procedures and aircraft limitations.

    Requirement. Conduct NATOPS closed book examination.

    Performance Standard. Achieve a minimum score of 3.3 on the closed book examination.

    Prerequisite. ACAD-6000

ACAD-6002 1.0   365   B,R,M   E

    Goal. The NATOPS oral examination shall consist of, but not be limited to the question bank. The instructor may draw upon their experience to propose questions of a direct and positive manner and in no way be opinionated to evaluate the 2nd Loadmaster's knowledge of the concerning normal/emergency procedures, aircraft limitations, and performance.

    Requirement. Conduct NATOPS oral examination.

    Performance Standard. Achieve a minimum grade of qualified on the oral examination.

    Prerequisite. ACAD-6000 and ACAD-6001

ACAD-6005   1.0   365   B,R,M   E

    Goal. CRM ground instruction in accordance with applicable directives and instructions.

    Requirement. Conduct CRM evaluation.

    Performance Standard. Demonstrate satisfactory knowledge of CRM 2LM princinciples and their application.

ACAD-6006   1.0   30   B,R,M   E

    Goal. Monthly emergency procedures exam.

    Requirement. Conduct a monthly emergency procedures exam per NAVMC 3500.14.

    Performance Standard. Achieve a passing grade on monthly emergency procedures exam.

ACAD-6007   1.0   90   B,R,M   (N)   E   S/A   1 C-9B

    Goal. Emergency procedure review.

    Requirement. This event will review C-9B emergency procedures and fulfills the requirement of quarterly emergency procedures simulator training per NAVMC 3500.14. This event can be accomplished in the aircraft while airborne or on the deck.

    Performance Standard. Comply with C-9B NFM emergency procedures.

4.21.2   NATOPS Evaluations (NTPS)

4.21.2.1 Purpose. Provide annual NATOPS and CRM evaluation flights.

NTPS-6100   2.0   365   B,R,M   (N)   E   A/S   1 C-9B

    Goal. Conduct annual NATOPS evaluation.

Requirement. Proficiency in the utilization of all aspects of the C-9B. The proficiency expected by the evaluator in this flight shall be commensurate with the experience of the 2nd Loadmaster under evaluation.

Performance Standard. The performance expected by the evaluator in this flight shall be commensurate with the experience level of the 2nd Loadmaster under evaluation.

Prerequisite. ACAD-6000, ACAD-6001, and ACAD-6002 within 60 days preceding this event. DESG-6200.

NTPS-6101   1.0   365   B,R,M   (N)   E   A/S   1 C-9B

Goal. Conduct annual CRM evaluation.

Requirement. Perform initial/annual CRM flight evaluation per applicable directives. May be flown in conjunction with annual NATOPS evaluation flight.

Performance Standard. Performance standards will be according to the C-9B NFM.

Prerequisite. ACAD-6005

4.21.3   Designation Flights (DESG)

4.21.3.1 Purpose. To provide an evaluation flight for designation as a 2LM.

4.21.3.2 General. 2LMUI will successfully complete a flight evaluation administered by a designated NATOPS Transport Safety Specialist Instructor.

DESG-6200   3.0   *   B,R   (N*)   E   A   1 C-9B

Goal. 2LMUI evaluation flight. 2LMUI to demonstrate the ability to meet NATOPS qualification per Chapter 18 NATOPS evaluation criteria. The flight evaluation is designed to measure with maximum objectivity the degree of standardization demonstrated by the 2LMUI and to ensure safety of flight.

Requirement

Brief/Discuss

The 2LMUI should be prepared to brief/discuss all previously introduced material.

Review

All previously introduced training shall be covered with particular attention given to NATOPS and emergency procedures.

Performance Standard. The 2LMUI Check should emphasize only those areas that are germane to the 2nd Loadmaster duties and demonstrated performance required to safely execute these duties.

Prerequisite. ACAD-6000, ACAD-6001, and ACAD-6002 within 60 days preceding this event. 1000 and 2000 series complete. Ground School complete.

4.22   T&R ATTAIN AND MAINTAIN SYLLABUS MATRICES

VMR-1 C-9B
2ND LOADMASTER
CORE/MISSION/CORE PLUS ATTAIN & MAINTAIN MATRIX

CORE SKILLS (2000 PHASE)

T&R EVENT INFORMATION				ATTAIN PROFICIENCY				MAINTAIN PROFICIENCY		PREREQUISITES	CHAINING
				BASIC POI		REFRESHER POI		MAINTAIN POI			
T&R DESCRIPTION	STAGE	CODE	RE FLY	STAGE	CODE	STAGE	CODE	STAGE	CODE		
Pas Responsibilities	PFAM	2100	*	PFAM	2100					1302	
Passenger Review	PFAM	2101R	365	PFAM	2101R	PFAM	2101R	PFAM	2101R	2100	
VIP Responsibilities	VFAM	2200	*	VFAM	2200					1302	
VIP Review	VFAM	2201R	365	VFAM	2201R	VFAM	2201R	VFAM	2201R	2200	2101

MISSION SKILLS (3000 PHASE)

T&R EVENT INFORMATION				ATTAIN PROFICIENCY				MAINTAIN PROFICIENCY		PREREQUISITES	CHAINING
				BASIC POI		REFRESHER POI		MAINTAIN POI			
T&R DESCRIPTION	STAGE	CODE	RE FLY	STAGE	CODE	STAGE	CODE	STAGE	CODE		
Passenger Mission	OSA	3100R	180	OSA	3100R	OSA	3100R	OSA	3100R	6200	3200,2101
Cargo Mission	ALS	3200R	180	ALS	3200R	ALS	3200R	ALS	3200R	6200	3100

CORE PLUS SKILLS (4000 PHASE)

T&R DESCRIPTION	STAGE	CODE	RE FLY	STAGE	CODE	STAGE	CODE	STAGE	CODE	PREREQUISITES	CHAINING
Intl/Trans Resp	IFAM	4000	*	IFAM	2300					1302	
Intl/Trans Rev	IFAM	4001R	365	IFAM	2301R	IFAM	2301R	IFAM	2301R	4000	

4.23   T&R SYLLABUS MATRIX

VMR-1 2ND LOADMASTER T&R MATRIX

STAGE	TRNG CODE	T&R DESCRIPTION	POI	DEVICE E	DEVICE # OF A/C	CON	RE FLY	# OF ACAD	ACAD TIME	# OF SIM	SIM TIME	# OF FLTS	FLT TIME	PREREQUISITE	NOTES	CHAINING	EVENT CONV
		CORE SKILL INTRODUCTION TRAINING (1000 PHASE EVENTS)															
		SIMULATOR (SIM)															
FAM	1300	Cabin Intro	B		A	1	(N*)	*	0	0.0	0	0.0	1	2.0	Water Survival/Flt Phy		
FAM	1301	Servicing Intro	B		A	1	(N*)	*	0	0.0	0	0.0	1	2.0	1300		
FAM	1302	Intro EPs	B,R		A	1	(N*)	*	0	0.0	0	0.0	1	2.0	1301		
		TOTAL FAM STAGE						0	0.0	0	0.0	3	6.0				
		TOTAL CORE SKILL INTRODUCTION PHASE (1000 PHASE)						0	0.0	0	0.0	3	6.0				
		CORE SKILL TRAINING (2000 PHASE EVENTS)															
		PASSENGER FAM (PFAM)															
PFAM	2100	Passenger FAM	B		A	1	(N*)	*	0	0.0	0	0.0	1	2.0	1302		
PFAM	2101	Passenger FAM Review	B,R,M		A	1	(N*)	365	0	0.0	0	0.0	1	2.0	2100		
		TOTAL PFAM STAGE						0	0.0	0	0.0	2	4.0				
		VIP FAM (VFAM)															
VFAM	2200	VIP FAM	B		A	1	(N*)	*	0	0.0	0	0.0	1	2.0	1302		
VFAM	2201	VIP FAM Review	B,R,M		A	1	(N*)	365	0	0.0	0	0.0	1	2.0	2200	2101	
		TOTAL VFAM STAGE						0	0.0	0	0.0	2	4.0				
		TOTAL CORE SKILL PHASE (2000 PHASE)						0	0.0	0	0.0	4	8.0				
		MISSION SKILL TRAINING (3000 PHASE)															
		OPERATIONAL AIRLIFT SUPPORT (OSA)															
OSA	3100	Passenger Mission	B,R,M		A	1	(N*)	180	0	0.0	0	0.0	1	2.0	6200	3200,2101	
		TOTAL OAS STAGE						0	0.0	0	0.0	1	2.0				
		AIR LOGISTICS SUPPORT (ALS)															
ALS	3200	Cargo Mission	B,R,M		A	1	(N*)	180	0	0.0	0	0.0	1	2.0	6200	3100	
		TOTAL ALS STAGE						0	0.0	0	0.0	1	2.0				
		TOTAL MISSION SKILL PHASE (3000 PHASE)						0	0.0	0	0.0	2	4.0				
		CORE PLUS TRAINING (4000 PHASE)															
		INTERNATIONAL FAM (IFAM)															
IFAM	4000	Intl/Trans FAM	B		A	1	(N*)	*	0	0.0	0	0.0	1	3.0	1302		
IFAM	4001	Intl/Trans FAM Review	B,R,M		A	1	(N*)	365	0	0.0	0	0.0	1	3.0	4000		
		TOTAL IFAM STAGE						0	0.0	0	0.0	2	6.0				
		TOTAL MISSION SKILL PHASE (4000 PHASE)						0	0.0	0	0.0	2	6.0				
		TOTAL 1000, 2000, & 3000 PHASE						0	0.0	0	0.0	11	24.0				

Enclosure (1)

VMR-1 2ND LOADMASTER T&R MATRIX

STAGE	TRNG CODE	T&R DESCRIPTION	POI	DEVICE E	# OF A/C	CON	RE FLX	# OF ACAD	ACAD TIME	# OF SIM	SIM TIME	# OF FLTS	FLT TIME	PREREQUISITE	NOTES	CHAINING	EVENT CONV
		INSTRUCTOR TRAINING (5000 PHASE EVENTS)															
		INSTRUCTOR TRAINING (IUT)															
IUT	5100	Instructor Intro	B,R	E	A	1	(N*)	*	0	0.0	0	0.0	1	3.0	6200,4001, 100 hrs in C-9B			
IUT	5101	Instructor Eval	B,R	E	A	1	(N*)	*	0	0.0	0	0.0	1	3.0	5100			
IUT	5102	NATOPS Eval Flight	B,R	E	A	1	(N*)	*	0	0.0	0	0.0	1	3.0	5101			
		TOTAL IUT STAGE						0	0.0	0	0.0	3	9.0				
		INSTRUCTOR TRAINING (5000 PHASE EVENTS) TOTAL						0	0.0	0	0.0	3	9.0				
		REQUIREMENT, QUALIFICATIONS, AND DESIGNATIONS (RQD) (6000 PHASE)															
		RQD ACADEMICS (ACAD)															
ACAD	6000	NATOPS Open Exam	B,R,M	E				365	1	1.0	0	0.0	0	0.0				
ACAD	6001	NATOPS Closed Exam	B,R,M	E				365	1	1.0	0	0.0	0	0.0				
ACAD	6002	NATOPS Oral Exam	B,R,M	E				365	1	1.0	0	0.0	0	0.0	6000			
ACAD	6005	CRM Ground Class	B,R,M	E				365	1	1.0	0	0.0	0	0.0	6000,6001			
ACAD	6006	Monthly EP Exam	B,R,M	E				30	1	1.0	0	0.0	0	0.0				
ACAD	6007	90 EP Review	B,R,M	E	S/A	1		90	1	1.0	0	0.0	0	0.0				
		TOTAL ACAD STAGE						6	6.0	0	0.0	0	0.0				
		NATOPS															
NTPS	6100	NATOPS Evaluation	B,R,M	E	A/S	1	(N)	365	0	0.0	0	0.0	1	2.0	6000,6001,6002			
NTPS	6101	CRM Flight Evaluation	B,R,M	E	A/S	1	(N)	365	0	0.0	0	0.0	1	1.0	6005			
		NATOPS TOTAL						0	0.0	0	0.0	2	3.0				
		T3P, T2P, TAC DESIGNATIONS (DESG)															
DESG	6200	2LM Designation	B,R	E	A	1	(N*)	*	0	0.0	0	0.0	1	3.0				
		TOTAL DESG STAGE						0	0.0	0	0.0	1	3.0				
		RQD TOTAL (6000 PHASE)						6	6.0	0	0.0	3	6.0				
		TOTAL 5000,6000 STAGES						6	6.0	0	0.0	6	15.0				
		TOTAL 2000,3000,4000,5000,6000 STAGES						6	6.0	0	0.0	17	39.0				

CHAPTER 4

2ND LOADMASTER

4.0   INDIVIDUAL TRAINING AND READINESS REQUIREMENTS. This T&R syllabus is based on specific goals and performance standards designed to ensure individual proficiency in Core, Mission, and Core Plus Skills. The goal of this chapter is to develop individual and unit war fighting capabilities.

4.1   TRAINING PROGRESSION MODEL. This model represents the recommended training progression for the average C-9B 2nd Loadmaster (2LM). Units should use the model as a guide to generate individual training plans.

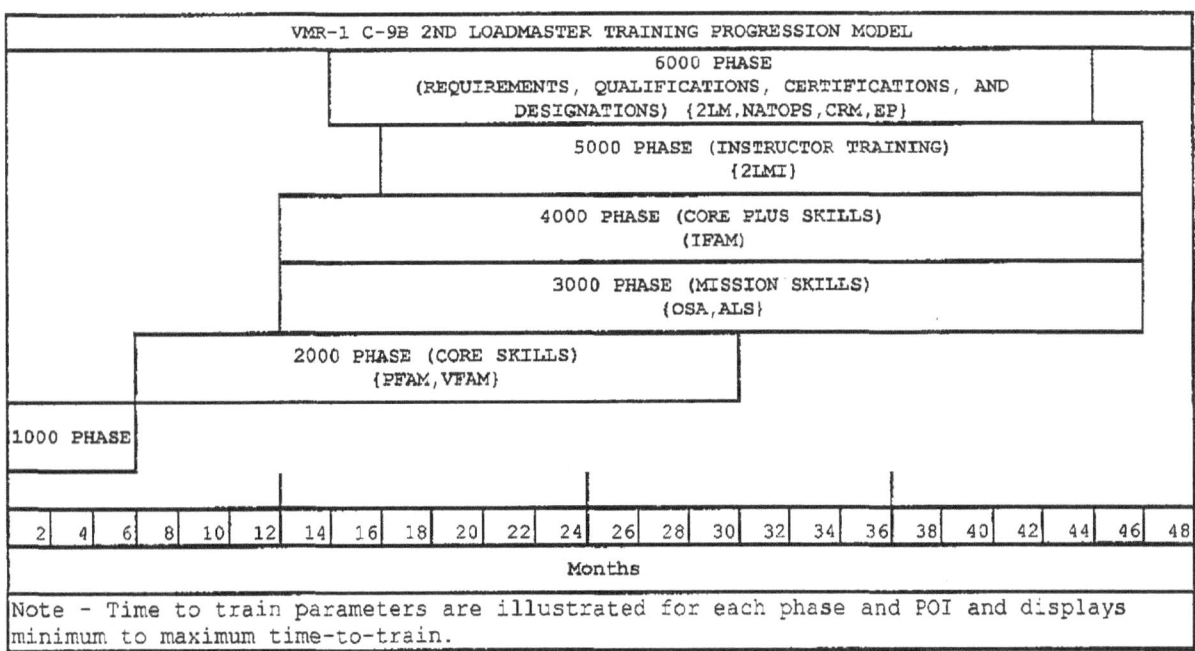

4.2   ABBREVIATIONS

VMR-1 C-9B 2ND LOADMASTER	
CORE/MISSION/CORE PLUS SKILL ABBREVIATIONS	
CORE SKILLS (2000 Phase)	
FAM	Familiarization
PFAM	Passenger Familiarization
VFAM	VIP Familiarization
MISSION SKILLS (3000 Phase)	
OSA	Operational Support Airlift
ALS	Air Logistics Support
CORE PLUS SKILLS (4000 Phase)	
IFAM	International/Transoceanic Familiarization
INSTRUCTOR (5000 Phase)	
2LMI	Second Loadmaster Instructor
QUALIFICATIONS AND DESIGNATIONS (6000 Phase)	
ACAD	Academics
NTPS	NATOPS
2LM	Second Loadmaster
EP	Emergency Procedures

4.3   DEFINITIONS

TERM	DEFINITION
Core Model	The Core Model is the basic foundation or standardized format by which all T&Rs are constructed. The Core Model provides the capability of quantifying both unit and individual training requirements and measuring readiness. This is accomplished by linking community Mission Statements, Mission Essential Task Lists, Output Standards, Core Skill Proficiency Requirements and Combat Leadership Matrices
Core Skill	Fundamental, environmental, or conditional capabilities required to perform basic functions. These basic functions serve as tactical enablers that allow crews to progress to the more complex Mission Skills. Primarily 2000 Phase events but may be introduced in the 1000 Phase.
Mission Skill	Mission Skills enable a unit to execute a specific MET. They are comprised of advanced event(s) that are focused on MET performance and draw upon the knowledge, aeronautical abilities, and situational awareness developed during Core Skill training. 3000 Phase events.
Core Plus Skill	Training events that can be theater specific or that have a low likelihood of occurrence. They may be Fundamental, environmental, or conditional capabilities required to perform basic functions. 4000 Phase events.
Core Plus Mission	Training events that can be theater specific or that have a low likelihood of occurrence. They are comprised of advanced event(s) that are focused on Core Plus MET performance and draw upon the knowledge, aeronautical abilities, and situational awareness. 4000 Phase events.
Core Skill Proficiency (CSP)	CSP is a measure of training completion for 2000 Phase events. CSP is attained by executing all events listed in the Attain Table for each Core Skill. The individual must be simultaneously proficient in all events within that Core Skill to attain CSP.
Mission Skill Proficiency (MSP)	MSP is a measure of training completion for 3000 Phase events. MSP is attained by executing all events listed in the Attain Table for each Mission Skill. The individual must be simultaneously proficient in all events within that Mission Skill to attain MSP. MSP is directly related to Training Readiness.
Core Plus Skill Proficiency (CPSP)	CPSP is a measure of training completion for 4000 Phase "Skill" events. CPSP is attained by executing all events listed in the Attain Table for each Core Plus Skill. The individual must be simultaneously proficient in all events within that Core Plus Skill to attain CPSP
Core Plus Mission Proficiency (CPMP)	CPMP is a measure of training completion for 4000 Phase "Mission" events. CPMP is attained by executing all events listed in the Attain Table for each Core Plus Mission. The individual must be simultaneously proficient in all events within that Core Plus Mission to attain CPMP

4.4   INDIVIDUAL CORE/MISSION/CORE PLUS SKILL PROFICIENCY REQUIREMENTS

4.4.1   Management of individual CSP/MSP/CPSP/CPMP serves as the foundation for developing proficiency requirements in DRRS.

4.4.2   Individual CSP is a "Yes/No" status assigned to an individual by Core Skill. When an individual attains and maintains CSP in a Core Skill, the individual counts towards CMMR Unit CSP requirements for that Core Skill.

4.4.3   Proficiency is attained by individual Core/Mission/Core Plus Skill and the training events to be executed within that skill set are determined by POI assignment (Basic, Transition, Conversion, Series Conversion, or Refresher).

4.4.4   Once proficiency has been attained by Core/Mission/Core Plus Skill (by any POI assignment) then the individual maintains proficiency by executing those events within the maintain column. An individual maintains proficiency by individual Core/Mission/Core Plus Skill.

Note
Individuals may be attaining proficiency
in some Core/Mission/Core Plus Skills
while maintaining proficiency in other
Core/Mission/Core Plus Skills.

4.4.5   Once proficiency has been attained, should one lose proficiency in
an event in the maintain column, proficiency can be attained by demonstrating
proficiency in the event which was delinquent. Should an individual lose
proficiency in all events in the Maintain column by Core/Mission/Core Plus
Skill, the individual will be assigned to the Refresher POI for that
Core/Mission/Core Plus Skill. To regain proficiency for that
Core/Mission/Core Plus Skill the individual must demonstrate proficiency in
all R-coded events for that Core/Mission/Core Plus Skill.

VMR-1 C-9B 2ND LOADMASTER					
ATTAIN AND MAINTAIN CORE/MISSION/CORE PLUS PROFICIENCY MATRIX BY POI					
ATTAIN PROFICIENCY				MAINTAIN PROFICIENCY	
BASIC POI		REFRESHER POI		MAINTAIN POI	
CORE SKILL (2000 Phase)					
PFAM	2100	PFAM		PFAM	2101R
	2101R		2101R		
VFAM	2200	VFAM		VFAM	2201R
	2201R		2201R		
MISSION SKILL (3000 Phase)					
OSA	3100R	OSA	3100R	OSA	3100R
ALS	3200R	ALS	3200R	ALS	3200R
CORE PLUS SKILL (4000 Phase)					
IFAM	4000	IFAM		IFAM	4001R
	4001R		4001R		
S prefix and blue font = flown in simulator					
R suffix and Grey highlight = R-coded "Refresher" event					

4.5   CERTIFICATION, QUALIFICATION AND DESIGNATION TABLES. The tables
below delineate T&R events required to be completed to attain proficiency,
initial qualifications and designations. In addition to event requirements,
all required stage lectures, briefs, squadron training, prerequisites, and
other criteria shall be completed prior to completing final events.
Certification, qualification and designation letters signed by the Commanding
Officer shall be placed in Aircrew Performance Records (APR) and NATOPS. Loss
of proficiency in all qualification events causes the associated
qualification to be lost. Regaining a qualification requires completing all
R-coded syllabus events associated with that qualification.

4.5.1   INSTRUCTOR DESIGNATIONS

VMR-1 C-9B 2ND LOADMASTER INSTRUCTOR DESIGNATIONS (5000 Phase)	
INSTRUCTOR DESIGNATION	EVENTS
2LM ASSISTANT NATOPS INSTRUCTOR (2LM ANI)	5100,5101
2LM NATOPS EVALUATOR/INSTRUCTOR (2LM NE/NI)	5100,5101,5102

4.5.2   REQUIREMENTS, CERTIFICATIONS, QUALIFICATIONS, AND DESIGNATIONS

4.5.2.1   The tables below delineate T&R events required to be completed to
attain initial qualifications and designations. All stage lectures, briefs,
squadron training, prerequisites, and open and closed book NATOPS exams shall
be complete and graded prior to completing evaluation flights. Qualification
and designation letters signed by the Commanding Officer shall be placed in
individual NATOPS and APR jackets.

VMR-1 C-9B 2ND LOADMASTER	
REQUIREMENTS, CERTIFICATIONS, QUALIFICATIONS, AND DESIGNATIONS (R,C,Q,& D) [6000 Phase]	
R,C,Q,& D	EVENTS
QUALIFICATIONS	
NATOPS	6000,6001,6002,6100
CRM	6005,6101
DESIGNATIONS	
2LM	6100,6200

4.6   VMR-1 C-9B 2ND LOADMASTER PROGRAMS OF INSTRUCTION (POI). These tables reflect average time-to-train versus the minimum to maximum time-to-train parameters in the Training Progression Model.

4.6.1   2LM training and designation sets the foundation for follow-on training as a Loadmaster or Crew Chief. Designation as a 2LM is a requirement for a C-9B air crewman to be considered by the squadron Standardization Board for assignment to either the Loadmaster syllabus or Crew Chief syllabus.

4.6.2   Basic POI. A Basic 2nd Loadmaster (2LM) shall be defined as an individual who has no previous experience as a 2LM. The 2LM Under Instruction (2LMUI) shall be screened by the squadron Aircrew Screening Board and approved by the Commanding Officer prior to commencing this POI. Every effort should be made to conduct VIP training codes aboard actual VIP missions, however, it is permissible to conduct simulated VIP missions as required in order to continue the student through the syllabus. All decisions as to POI eligibility rest with the Commanding Officer. The 2LM Under Instruction shall be considered qualified to function as a qualified 2LM on both CONUS and OCONUS missions upon completion of the 2LM designation flight (DESG-6200). Upon completion of the 2LM designation, the 2LM must complete OSA-3100 and ALS-3200 under the supervision of an instructor prior to performing those duties individually. Additionally, the 2LM becomes eligible for consideration by the squadron Standardization Board for assignment to the Loadmaster or Crew Chief syllabus upon designation as a 2LM. The International/Trans Oceanic flights (IFAM 4000 and IFAM 4001) are established to ensure the 2LM has been exposed to Overwater/International procedures prior to assignment to the 2LM NATOPS Instructor/Evaluator Phases. As such, these flights shall be complete prior to commencing the 2LM Instructor or 2LM NATOPS Instructor/Evaluator syllabus.

VMR-1 C-9B 2ND LOADMASTER		
Basic POI		
Weeks	Phase of Instruction	Unit
1	Water Survival/Flight Physiology	NAWSTP
1	Ground Training	VMR-1
3	Core Skill Introduction (1000 Phase)	VMR-1
3	Core Skill (2000 Phase)	VMR-1
3	Mission Skill (3000 Phase)	VMR-1

4.6.3   Refresher POI. The 2LMUI must have flown in the capacity as a C-9B 2LM during the previous two years in order to be eligible for this refresher POI. The 2LMUI shall have been recommended by the squadron Standardization Board and approved by the Commanding Officer prior to commencing this refresher POI. All decisions as to POI eligibility rest with the Commanding Officer.

4.6.3.1   A 2LM who has been assigned to other duty preventing currency in the C-9B aircraft for a period exceeding 24 months is not eligible for Refresher

2LM training and must complete the basic POI prior to re-designation as a 2LM.

VMR-1 C-9B 2ND LOADMASTER Refresher POI		
Weeks	Phase of Instruction	Unit
1	Water Survival/Flight Physiology *	NAWSTP
2	Core Introduction (1000 Phase)	VMR-1
2	Core Skill (2000 Phase)	VMR-1
2	Mission Skill (3000 Phase)	VMR-1
* Required only if NAWSTP Swim Qualification is expired.		

4.6.4   POI FOR INSTRUCTOR 2ND LOADMASTER UNDER TRAINING (IUT). The 2LMIUT shall have been recommended by the squadron Standardization Board and approved by the Commanding Officer prior to commencing this POI. All decisions as to POI eligibility rest with the Commanding Officer. The 2LMIUT will complete IFAM-4000 and IFAM-4001 prior to assignment to the 2LM Instructor or 2LM NATOPS Instructor/Evaluator Training.

VMR-1 C-9B 2ND LOADMASTER Instructor POI		
Weeks	Phase of Instruction	Unit
1	2LM Instructor Training	VMR-1
1	2LM NATOPS Evaluator Training	VMR-1

4.7   SYLLABUS NOTES

4.7.1   Environmental Conditions Matrix

Environmental Conditions	
Code	Meaning
D	Shall be flown during hours of daylight: (by exception - there is no use of a symbol)
N*	Shall be flown during hours of darkness must be flown unaided
(N*)	May be flown during hours of darkness - If flown during hours of darkness must be flown unaided
Note - If the event is to be flown in the simulator the Simulator Instructor shall set the desired environmental conditions for the event.	

4.7.2   Device Matrix

DEVICE (Aviation Flying)	
Symbol	Meaning
A	Flown in aircraft
A/S	Aircraft preferred may be flown in simulator
S	Flown in simulator
S/A	Simulator preferred may be flown in aircraft
Note - If the event is to be flown in the simulator the Simulator Instructor shall set the desired environmental conditions for the event.	

4.7.3   Program of Instruction Matrix

PROGRAM OF INSTRUCTION MATRIX			
Program of Instruction (POI)	Symbol	Aviation Flying	Aviation Ground
Basic	B	Initial MOS/Skill Training	Initial MOS training
Refresher	R	DIFDEN to DIFOPS in same T/M/S	Return to community from non (MOS/Skill) associated tour
Maintain	M	All individuals who have attained CSP/MSP/CPP by initial POI assignment are re-assigned to the M POI to maintain proficiency.	
*Many communities will assign transition and conversion aircrew to the basic POI.			

4.7.4   Event Terms

EVENT TERMS	
TERM	**DESCR2LMITION**
Discuss	An explanation of systems, procedures, or maneuvers during the brief, in flight, or post flight. Student is responsible for knowledge of procedures.
Demonstrate	The description and performance of a particular maneuver/event by the instructor, observed by the 2LMUI/student. The 2LMUI/student is responsible for knowledge of the procedures prior to the demonstration of a required maneuver/student.
Introduce	The instructor may demonstrate a procedure or maneuver to a student, or may coach the 2LMUI through the maneuver without demonstration. The 2LMUI performs the procedures or maneuver with coaching as necessary. The 2LMUI is responsible for knowledge of the procedures.
Practice	The performance of a maneuver or procedure by the 2LMUI/student that may have been previously introduced in order to attain a specified level of performance.
Review	Demonstrated proficiency of a maneuver by the 2LMUI/student.
Evaluate	Any flight designed to evaluate aircrew standardization that does not fit another category such as SARCK, HACCK, T2PCK, etc.
E-Coded	This term means that documentation (ATF) is required each time the event is logged. Requires evaluation by a certified standardization instructor (NATOPS I, WTI, INST Evaluator etc.)

4.8   CORE SKILL INTRODUCTION FRS ACADEMIC PHASE (0000 Phase). There are no 0000 phase events in the C-9B T&R manual. However, the squadron training listed below is required.

4.8.1   The following one-week ground training syllabus is intended as squadron-level training for 2nd Loadmasters during initial qualification. Refresher 2nd Loadmasters are exempt from this ground training syllabus. This ground training may be conducted concurrently with the flight training syllabus. However, the ground training syllabus must be complete prior to the designation flight (DESG-6200).

General aircraft description
Aircraft systems
Aircraft emergency equipment and systems
Emergency procedures
2LM procedures and responsibilities
Personal fying equipment requirements
Aircraft mission
NATOPS open and closed book examinations

4.9   CORE SKILL INTRODUCTION PHASE (1000). The core skill introduction phase is designed to familiarize the 2LMUI with C-9B ground servicing, normal procedures, CRM, systems operation and limitations, and emergency procedures.

4.10   CORE SKILL INTRODUCTION STAGES (1000)

PARAGRAPH	STAGE
4.10.1	Familiarization (FAM)

4.10.1   Familiarization Flights (FAM)

4.10.1.1   Purpose. Familiarize the 2LMUI with the C-9B aircraft. Introduce NATOPS procedures, operation and servicing of aircraft equipment, and all duties and procedures required of a qualified 2LM.

4.10.1.2   Crew Requirements. TAC, T2P, CC, LM, 2LMI, 2LMUI

FAM-1300   2.0   *   B   (N*)   A   1 C-9B

    Goal. Cabin facilities introduction.

    Requirement

       Discuss/Demonstrate/Introduce

         Preflight responsibilities
         Operation of the heads
         Coffee makers
         Freezer
         Refrigerator and ovens
         Duties of the 2LM during the flight
         Post flight duties
       Review
         Ground training material

    Performance Standard. Student will have a general understanding of the responsibilities of a 2LM.

    Prerequisite. Nomination by Aircrew Screening Board, approval of Commanding Officer, successful completion of water survival and flight physiology.

FAM-1301   2.0   *   B   (N*)   A   1 C-9B

    Goal. Servicing introduction and review of previous instruction.

    Requirement

       Discuss/Demonstrate/Introduce

         Servicing of heads
         Maintenance of servicing carts
         Review of holding tank capabilities
         Servicing of fresh water cart
         Capacities of the holding tank
       Review
         Previously covered material

    Performance Standard. 2LMUI will demonstrate proficiency in all previously covered training and have a general knowledge of all items covered pertaining to FAM-1300.

    Prerequisite. FAM-1300

FAM-1302   2.0   *   B,R   (N*)   A   1 C-9B

    Goal. Introduce the 2LM responses/actions required during each ground and airborne emergency.

    Requirement

       Discuss/Demonstrate/Introduce

         Rapid depressurization/emergency descent
         Fuselage fire
         Cabin smoke/fume elimination
         In-flight hazardous spill
         Crash landing/abnormal landing/ditching
         Refilling of walk around oxygen bottles
         Location and use of all emergency equipment
       Review
         Previously covered material

    Performance Standard. 2LMUI will demonstrate proficiency regarding all previous training and be introduced to new material. Student should be able to demonstrate all asterisk emergency procedure items which involve the 2LM position.

Prerequisite. FAM-1301

4.11   CORE SKILL PHASE (2000)

4.11.1   General

Core Skill Phase in the C-9B introduces the 2LMUI to the requirements and responsibilities when carrying passengers, cargo, and VIPs (Code 7 and higher).

4.12   CORE SKILL INTRODUCTION STAGES (2000)

PARAGRAPH	STAGE
4.12.1	Passenger Familiarization (PFAM)
4.12.2	VIP Familiarization (VFAM)

4.12.1   Passenger Familiarization (PFAM)

4.12.1.1 Purpose. Instruct the 2LMUI in proper procedures for passenger handling.

4.12.1.2 Crew Requirements. TAC, T2P, LM, 2LMI, 2LMUI

PFAM-2100   2.0   *   B   (N*)   A   1 C-9B

> Goal. 2LMUI will be instructed on 2LM responsibilities on a passenger flight.
>
> Requirement
>> Discuss
>>> Passenger and baggage handling
>>> Responsibilities on turn-around
>>> Handling, storing, preparing, and serving in-flight meals
>>> RON procedures
>> Demonstrate/Introduce
>>> Passenger and baggage handling
>>> Responsibilities on turn-around
>>> Handling, storing, preparing, and serving in-flight meals
>>> RON procedures
>> Review
>>> Previously covered material as necessary
>
> Performance Standard. Student will demonstrate proficiency in all previously covered training and have a general knowledge of all items covered pertaining to FAM-1301.
>
> Prerequisite. FAM-1302

PFAM-2101   2.0   365   B,R,M   (N*)   A   1 C-9B

> Goal. 2LMUI will demonstrate proficiency in all aspects of duties and responsibilities on a passenger flight.
>
> Requirement
>> Discuss
>>> Passenger and baggage handling
>>> Responsibilities on turn-around

Handling, storing, preparing, and serving in-flight meals
RON procedures

Review

Passenger and baggage handling
Responsibilities on turn-around
Handling, storing, preparing, and serving in-flight meals
RON procedures
Previously covered material as necessary

Performance Standard. 2LMUI will demonstrate proficiency in all previously covered training and have a general knowledge of all items covered pertaining to FAM-2101.

Prerequisite. PFAM-2100

4.12.2 VIP Familiarization (VFAM)

4.12.2.1 Purpose. Instruct the 2LMUI in the proper procedures when carrying a VIP passenger.

4.12.2.2 Crew Requirements. TAC, T2P, LM, 2LMI, 2LMUI

VFAM-2200   2.0   *   B   (N*)   A   1 C-9B

Goal. 2LMUI will be instructed on responsibilities on a VIP flight.

Requirement

Discuss
Unique procedures during the flight
Uniform and appearance during the flight

Demonstrate/Introduce
Unique procedures during the flight
Uniform and appearance during the flight

Review
Previously covered material as necessary

Performance Standard. Student will demonstrate proficiency in all previously covered training and have a general knowledge of all items covered pertaining to VFAM-2200.

Prerequisite. FAM-1302

VFAM-2201   2.0   365   B,R,M   (N*)   A   1 C-9B

Goal. 2LMUI will demonstrate proficiency in all aspects of duties and responsibilities on a VIP flight.

Requirement

Discuss
Unique procedures during the flight
Uniform and appearance during the flight

Review
Unique procedures during the flight
Uniform and appearance during the flight
Previously covered material as necessary

Performance Standard. 2LMUI will demonstrate proficiency in all previously covered training and conduct VIP procedures with minimal supervision from the 2LM instructor.

Prerequisite. VFAM-2200

NAVMC 3500.31A
22 Nov 11

4.13   MISSION SKILLS PHASE (3000)

4.13.1 General. The Mission Skill Phase is designed to familiarize the
2LMUI with the unique missions and challenges associated with the VMR-1, C-
9B. Mission Skills are designed to fulfill the requirements of the C-9B
Mission Essential Task List as defined by the associated Marine Corps Task
(MCT).

4.14   MISSION SKILL STAGES (3000)

PARAGRAPH	STAGE
4:14.1	Operational Support Airlift (OSA)
4.14.2	Air Logistics Support (ALS)

4.14.1 Operational Support Airlift (OSA)

4.14.1.1 Purpose. This event is designed to fulfill the requirement set in
MCT 1.3.4.1.2, conduct OSA.

4.14.1.2 General. It is understood that many missions will be a combination
of both passenger and cargo transportation and both codes will be used when
filling out the NAVFLIR. Both codes are made available for flights that
clearly fall into a single category.

4.14.1.3 Crew Requirement. Full mission crew.

OSA-3100   2.0   180   B,R,M   (N*)   A   1   C-9B
    Goal. Introduce the 2LMUI to the JOSAC/ASM passenger mission or
    provide continued update to the skills of the 2LM while performing the
    passenger mission.
    Requirement. 2LM/2LMUI will execute a JOSAC/ASM passenger mission and
    perform all 2LM flight related duties safely and proficiently.
    Performance Standard. 2LM/2LMUI will safely conduct all duties related
    to the JOSAC passenger mission with proficiency.
    Prerequisite. DESG-6200

4.14.2 Air Logistics Support (ALS)

4.14.2.1 Purpose. This event is designed to fulfill the requirement set in
MMC 4.3.8, conduct ALS.

4.14.2.2 General. It is understood that many missions will be a combination
of both passenger and cargo transportation and both codes will be used when
filling out the NAVFLIR. Both codes are made available for flights that
clearly fall into a single category.

4.14.2.3 Crew Requirement. Full mission crew.

ALS-3200   2.0   180   B,R,M   (N*)   A   1   C-9B
    Goal. Introduce the 2LMUI to the C-9B cargo mission or provide
    continued update to the 2LM skills used while performing the cargo
    missions.
    Requirement. 2LM/2LMUI will execute a JOSAC cargo mission and perform
    all 2LM flight related duties safely and proficiently.
    Performance Standard. 2LM/2LMUI will safely conduct all duties related
    to the JOSAC cargo mission with proficiency
    Prerequisite. DESG-6200

4.15   CORE PLUS SKILL PHASE (4000)

4.15.1   General. Core Skill Plus Phase in the C-9B introduces the 2LMUI to the requirements and responsibilities when flying internationally.

4.16   CORE PLUS SKILL STAGES (4000)

PARAGRAPH	STAGE
4.16.1	International/Tansoceanic Familiarization

4.16.1   International/Transoceanic Familiarization (IFAM)

4.16.1.1 Purpose. To instruct the 2LMUI in procedures required when flying on IFAM flights. This phase is established to prepare the 2LMUI for follow-on instruction in the 2LM Instructor and 2LM NATOPS Evaluator Phases.

4.16.1.2 Crew Requirements. TAC, T2P, LM, 2LMI, 2LMUI

IFAM-4000   3.0   *   B   (N*)   A   1 C-9B

    Goal. 2LMUI will be instructed on responsibilities on an International/Transoceanic flight.

    Requirement

      Discuss

        Over water passenger brief
        Location and use of all rafts, slides and life vests
        Ditching procedures
        International procedures

      Demonstrate/Introduce

        Over water passenger brief
        Location and use of all rafts, slides and life vests
        Ditching procedures
        International procedures

      Review

        Previously covered material as necessary

    Performance Standard. 2LMUI will demonstrate proficiency in all previously covered training and have a general knowledge of all items covered pertaining to IFAM-2300.

    Prerequisite. FAM-1302

IFAM-4001   3.0   365   B,R,M   (N*)   A   1 C-9B

    Goal. 2LM/2LMUI will demonstrate proficiency in all aspects of duties and responsibilities on an IFAM flight.

    Requirement

      Discuss

        Over water passenger brief
        Location and use of all rafts, slides and life vests
        Ditching procedures
        International procedures

      Review

        Over water passenger brief
        Location and use of all rafts, slides and life vests
        Ditching procedures

International procedures

Performance Standard. 2LM/2LMUI will demonstrate proficiency in all previously covered training and conduct all overwater related 2LM duties with minimal supervision. Student needs to be capable of independently conducting all 2LM duties related to IFAM flight.

Prerequisite. IFAM-2300

4.17   INSTRUCTOR TRAINING PHASE (5000)

4.17.1   General. The instructor training phase is designed to provide the squadron with a cadre of qualified instructors needed to ensure quality training at all times.

PARAGRAPH	STAGE
4.18.1	Instructor Under Training (IUT)

4.18   Instructor Training Stages (5000)

4.18.1   Instructor Under Training (IUT)

4.18.1.1 Purpose. Develop qualified 2nd Loadmaster instructors with the ability to teach all phases of C-9B flight and mission requirements.

4.18.1.2 General. A 2LMI is qualified to instruct in all phases of aircraft operations. A 2LM must have 100 hours (waiverable by the Commanding Officer) in the C-9B before being recommended for the instructor syllabus.

4.18.1.2 Crew Requirements. TAC, T2P, CC, LM, 2LMI/E, 2LMIUT, 2LM

IUT-5100   3.0   *   B,R   (N*)   E   A   1 C-9B

Goal. Instruction introduction.

Requirement

Brief/Discuss

Conduct of training flight
Instructional techniques
T&R and syllabus evaluation forms

Review

The 2LMI shall observe a 2LMIUT instruct a 2LMUI on a syllabus flight. The 2LMI shall demonstrate emphasis upon evaluating the 2LMIUT's instruction of aircraft servicing, passenger handling, and emergency procedures.

Performance Standard. 2LMIUT should have a solid knowledge of aircraft and 2LM responsibilities during all aspects of ground and flight operations.

Prerequisite. DESG-6200, IFAM-4001, 100 hours in C-9B as a 2LM

IUT-5101   3.0   *   B,R   (N*)   E   A   1 C-9B

Goal. Qualify the 2LM as a 2LM ANI.

Requirement

Discuss

Conduct of evaluation flight
Review all 2LM/2LMI ground and flight responsibilities, publications, and required documentation

Review. The 2LM shall perform all duties of a 2LMI on a flight with a 2LMUI while being evaluated by a 2LM NATOPS Instructor/Evaluator.

Performance Standard. 2LM will demonstrate the requisite maturity, instructional ability, and standardization expected of a 2LMI.

Prerequisite. IUT-5100

IUT-5102   3.0   *   B,R   (N*) E   A   1 C-9B

Goal. Qualify the 2LMI as a NATOPS Instructor/Evaluator 2LM NI/NE.

Requirement

Discuss

Conduct of evaluation flight
Responsibilities of the 2LM NI/NE

Review

The 2LM ANI shall be evaluated by a 2LM NATOPS Evaluator while instructing a 2LMUI
The 2LM ANI being evaluated must display the maturity, integrity, and knowledge of the aircraft required to conduct a NATOPS evaluation

Performance Standard. Student will demonstrate the requisite maturity, instructional ability, and standardization expected of a 2LM NI/NE.

Prerequisite. IUT-5101

4.19   REQUIREMENTS, CERTIFICATIONS, QUALIFICATIONS, AND DESIGNATIONS (RCQD) PHASE (6000)

4.19.1   General. The 6000 phase encompasses the events required to maintain currency with all certifications, qualifications, and designations.

4.20   REQUIREMENTS, CERTIFICATIONS, QUALIFICATIONS, AND DESIGNATIONS (RCQD) STAGES (6000)

PARAGRAPH	STAGE
4.21.1	Academics (ACAD)
4.21.2	NATOPS (NTPS)
4.21.3	Designations (DESG)

4.21.1   Academics (ACAD)

4.21.1.1 Purpose. To complete the academic requirements for subsequent annual evaluation flights.

ACAD-6000   1.0   365   B,R,M   E

Goal. The NATOPS open book examination shall consist of, but not be limited to the question bank. The purpose of the open book examination is to evaluate the 2nd Loadmaster's knowledge of the appropriate publications and the aircraft.

Performance Standard. Achieve a minimum score of 3.5 on the open book examination.

ACAD-6001   1.0   365   B,R,M   E

> Goal. The purpose of the NATOPS closed book examination is to evaluate the 2nd Loadmaster's knowledge of the concerning normal/emergency procedures and aircraft limitations.
>
> Requirement. Conduct NATOPS closed book examination.
>
> Performance Standard. Achieve a minimum score of 3.3 on the closed book examination.
>
> Prerequisite. ACAD-6000

ACAD-6002 1.0   365   B,R,M   E

> Goal. The NATOPS oral examination shall consist of, but not be limited to the question bank. The instructor may draw upon their experience to propose questions of a direct and positive manner and in no way be opinionated to evaluate the 2nd Loadmaster's knowledge of the concerning normal/emergency procedures, aircraft limitations, and performance.
>
> Requirement. Conduct NATOPS oral examination.
>
> Performance Standard. Achieve a minimum grade of qualified on the oral examination.
>
> Prerequisite. ACAD-6000 and ACAD-6001

ACAD-6005   1.0   365   B,R,M   E

> Goal. CRM ground instruction in accordance with applicable directives and instructions.
>
> Requirement. Conduct CRM evaluation.
>
> Performance Standard. Demonstrate satisfactory knowledge of CRM 2LM princinciples and their application.

ACAD-6006   1.0   30   B,R,M   E

> Goal. Monthly emergency procedures exam.
>
> Requirement. Conduct a monthly emergency procedures exam per NAVMC 3500.14.
>
> Performance Standard. Achieve a passing grade on monthly emergency procedures exam.

ACAD-6007   1.0   90   B,R,M   (N)   E   S/A   1 C-9B

> Goal. Emergency procedure review.
>
> Requirement. This event will review C-9B emergency procedures and fulfills the requirement of quarterly emergency procedures simulator training per NAVMC 3500.14. This event can be accomplished in the aircraft while airborne or on the deck.
>
> Performance Standard. Comply with C-9B NFM emergency procedures.

4.21.2   NATOPS Evaluations (NTPS)

4.21.2.1 Purpose. Provide annual NATOPS and CRM evaluation flights.

NTPS-6100   2.0   365   B,R,M   (N)   E   A/S   1 C-9B

> Goal. Conduct annual NATOPS evaluation.

Requirement. Proficiency in the utilization of all aspects of the C-9B. The proficiency expected by the evaluator in this flight shall be commensurate with the experience of the 2nd Loadmaster under evaluation.

Performance Standard. The performance expected by the evaluator in this flight shall be commensurate with the experience level of the 2nd Loadmaster under evaluation.

Prerequisite. ACAD-6000, ACAD-6001, and ACAD-6002 within 60 days preceding this event. DESG-6200.

NTPS-6101   1.0   365   B,R,M   (N)   E   A/S   1 C-9B

Goal. Conduct annual CRM evaluation.

Requirement. Perform initial/annual CRM flight evaluation per applicable directives. May be flown in conjunction with annual NATOPS evaluation flight.

Performance Standard. Performance standards will be according to the C-9B NFM.

Prerequisite. ACAD-6005

4.21.3   Designation Flights (DESG)

4.21.3.1 Purpose. To provide an evaluation flight for designation as a 2LM.

4.21.3.2 General. 2LMUI will successfully complete a flight evaluation administered by a designated NATOPS Transport Safety Specialist Instructor.

DESG-6200   3.0   *   B,R   (N*)   E   A   1 C-9B

Goal. 2LMUI evaluation flight. 2LMUI to demonstrate the ability to meet NATOPS qualification per Chapter 18 NATOPS evaluation criteria. The flight evaluation is designed to measure with maximum objectivity the degree of standardization demonstrated by the 2LMUI and to ensure safety of flight.

Requirement

   Brief/Discuss

      The 2LMUI should be prepared to brief/discuss all previously introduced material.

   Review

      All previously introduced training shall be covered with particular attention given to NATOPS and emergency procedures.

Performance Standard. The 2LMUI Check should emphasize only those areas that are germane to the 2nd Loadmaster duties and demonstrated performance required to safely execute these duties.

Prerequisite. ACAD-6000, ACAD-6001, and ACAD-6002 within 60 days preceding this event. 1000 and 2000 series complete. Ground School complete.

4.22   T&R ATTAIN AND MAINTAIN SYLLABUS MATRICES

VMR-1 C-9B
2ND LOADMASTER
CORE/MISSION/CORE PLUS ATTAIN & MAINTAIN MATRIX

CORE SKILLS (2000 PHASE)

T&R EVENT INFORMATION				ATTAIN PROFICIENCY				MAINTAIN PROFICIENCY		PREREQUISITES	CHAINING
				BASIC POI		REFRESHER POI		MAINTAIN POI			
T&R DESCRIPTION	STAGE	CODE	RE FLY	STAGE	CODE	STAGE	CODE	STAGE	CODE		
Pas Responsibilities	PFAM	2100	*	PFAM	2100					1302	
Passenger Review	PFAM	2101R	365	PFAM	2101R	PFAM	2101R	PFAM	2101R	2100	
VIP Responsibilities	VFAM	2200	*	VFAM	2200					1302	
VIP Review	VFAM	2201R	365	VFAM	2201R	VFAM	2201R	VFAM	2201R	2200	2101

MISSION SKILLS (3000 PHASE)

T&R EVENT INFORMATION				ATTAIN PROFICIENCY				MAINTAIN PROFICIENCY		PREREQUISITES	CHAINING
				BASIC POI		REFRESHER POI		MAINTAIN POI			
T&R DESCRIPTION	STAGE	CODE	RE FLY	STAGE	CODE	STAGE	CODE	STAGE	CODE		
Passenger Mission	OSA	3100R	180	OSA	3100R	OSA	3100R	OSA	3100R	6200	3200,2101
Cargo Mission	ALS	3200R	180	ALS	3200R	ALS	3200R	ALS	3200R	6200	3100

CORE PLUS SKILLS (4000 PHASE)

T&R DESCRIPTION	STAGE	CODE	RE FLY	STAGE	CODE	STAGE	CODE	STAGE	CODE	PREREQUISITES	CHAINING
Intl/Trans Resp	IFAM	4000	+	IFAM	2300					1302	
Intl/Trans Rev	IFAM	4001R	365	IFAM	2301R	IFAM	2301R	IFAM	2301R	4000	

4.23   T&R SYLLABUS MATRIX

VMR-1 2ND LOADMASTER T&R MATRIX

STAGE	TRNG CODE	T&R DESCRIPTION	POI E	DEVICE # OF A/C		CON	RE FLY	# OF ACAD	ACAD TIME OF	# OF SIM	SIM TIME OF	# OF SIM FLTS	FLT TIME	PREREQUISITE	NOTES	CHAINING	EVENT CONV
		CORE SKILL INTRODUCTION TRAINING (1000 PHASE EVENTS)															
		SIMULATOR (SIM)															
FAM	1300	Cabin Intro	B	A	1	(N*)	*	0	0.0	0	0.0	1	2.0	Water Survival/Flt Phy			
FAM	1301	Servicing Intro	B	A	1	(N*)	*	0	0.0	0	0.0	1	2.0	1300			
FAM	1302	Intro EPs	B,R	A	1	(N*)	*	0	0.0	0	0.0	1	2.0	1301			
		TOTAL FAM STAGE						0	0.0			3	6.0				
		TOTAL CORE SKILL INTRODUCTION PHASE (1000 PHASE)						0	0.0			3	6.0				
		CORE SKILL TRAINING (2000 PHASE EVENTS)															
		PASSENGER FAM (PFAM)															
PFAM	2100	Passenger FAM	B	A	1	(N*)	*	0	0.0	0	0.0	1	2.0	1302			
PFAM	2101	Passenger FAM Review	B,R,M	A	1	(N*)	365	0	0.0	0	0.0	1	2.0	2100			
		TOTAL PFAM STAGE						0	0.0			2	4.0				
		VIP FAM (VFAM)															
VFAM	2200	VIP FAM	B	A	1	(N*)	*	0	0.0	0	0.0	1	2.0	1302			
VFAM	2201	VIP FAM Review	B,R,M	A	1	(N*)	365	0	0.0	0	0.0	1	2.0	2200	2101		
		TOTAL VFAM STAGE						0	0.0			2	4.0				
		TOTAL CORE SKILL PHASE (2000 PHASE)						0	0.0			4	8.0				
		MISSION SKILL TRAINING (3000 PHASE)															
		OPERATIONAL AIRLIFT SUPPORT (OSA)															
OSA	3100	Passenger Mission	B,R,M	A	1	(N*)	180	0	0.0	0	0.0	1	2.0	6200		3200,2101	
		TOTAL OAS STAGE						0	0.0			1	2.0				
		AIR LOGISTICS SUPPORT (ALS)															
ALS	3200	Cargo Mission	B,R,M	A	1	(N*)	180	0	0.0	0	0.0	1	2.0	6200		3100	
		TOTAL ALS STAGE						0	0.0			1	2.0				
		TOTAL MISSION SKILL PHASE (3000 PHASE)						0	0.0			2	4.0				
		CORE PLUS TRAINING (4000 PHASE)															
		INTERNATIONAL FAM (IFAM)															
IFAM	4000	Intl/Trans FAM	B	A	1	(N*)	*	0	0.0	0	0.0	1	3.0	1302			
IFAM	4001	Intl/Trans FAM Review	B,R,M	A	1	(N*)	365	0	0.0	0	0.0	1	3.0	4000			
		TOTAL IFAM STAGE						0	0.0			2	6.0				
		TOTAL MISSION SKILL PHASE (4000 PHASE)						0	0.0			2	6.0				
		TOTAL 1000, 2000, & 3000 PHASE						0	0.0			11	24.0				

VMR-1 2ND LOADMASTER T&R MATRIX

INSTRUCTOR TRAINING (5000 PHASE EVENTS)

INSTRUCTOR UNDER TRAINING (IUT)

STAGE	TRNG CODE	T&R DESCR/LIMITATION	POI	DEVICE E	E	# OF A/C	CON	RE FLY	# OF ACAD	ACAD TIME	# OF SIM	SIM TIME	# OF FLTS	FLT TIME	PREREQUISITE	NOTES	CHAINING	EVENT CONV
IUT	5100	Instructor Intro	B,R	E	A	1	(N*)	*	0	0.0	0	0.0	1	3.0	6200,4001, 100 hrs in C-9B			
IUT	5101	Instructor Eval	B,R	E	A	1	(N*)	*	0	0.0	0	0.0	1	3.0	5100			
IUT	5102	NATOPS Eval Flight	B,R	E	A	1	(N*)	*	0	0.0	0	0.0	1	3.0	5101			
		TOTAL IUT STAGE							0	0.0	0	0.0	3	9.0				
		INSTRUCTOR TRAINING (5000 PHASE EVENTS) TOTAL							0	0.0	0	0.0	3	9.0				

REQUIREMENT, QUALIFICATIONS, AND DESIGNATIONS (RQD) (6000 PHASE)

RQD ACADEMICS (ACAD)

STAGE	TRNG CODE	T&R DESCR/LIMITATION	POI	DEVICE E	E	# OF A/C	CON	RE FLY	# OF ACAD	ACAD TIME	# OF SIM	SIM TIME	# OF FLTS	FLT TIME	PREREQUISITE	NOTES	CHAINING	EVENT CONV
ACAD	6000	NATOPS Open Exam	B,R,M	E				365	1	1.0	0	0.0	0	0.0				
ACAD	6001	NATOPS Closed Exam	B,R,M	E				365	1	1.0	0	0.0	0	0.0	6000			
ACAD	6002	NATOPS Oral Exam	B,R,M	E				365	1	1.0	0	0.0	0	0.0	6000,6001			
ACAD	6005	CRM Ground Class	B,R,M	E				365	1	1.0	0	0.0	0	0.0				
ACAD	6006	Monthly EP Exam	B,R,M	E				30	1	1.0	0	0.0	0	0.0				
ACAD	6007	90 EP Review	B,R,M	E	S/A	1		90	1	1.0	0	0.0	0	0.0				
		TOTAL ACAD STAGE							6	6.0	0	0.0	0	0.0				

NATOPS

STAGE	TRNG CODE	T&R DESCR/LIMITATION	POI	DEVICE E	E	# OF A/C	CON	RE FLY	# OF ACAD	ACAD TIME	# OF SIM	SIM TIME	# OF FLTS	FLT TIME	PREREQUISITE	NOTES	CHAINING	EVENT CONV
NTPS	6100	NATOPS Evaluation	B,R,M	E	A/S	1	(N)	365	0	0.0	0	0.0	1	2.0	6000,6001,6002			
NTPS	6101	CRM Flight Evaluation	B,R,M	E	A/S	1	(N)	365	0	0.0	0	0.0	1	1.0	6005			
		NATOPS TOTAL							0	0.0	0	0.0	2	3.0				

T3P, T2P, TAC DESIGNATIONS (DESG)

STAGE	TRNG CODE	T&R DESCR/LIMITATION	POI	DEVICE E	E	# OF A/C	CON	RE FLY	# OF ACAD	ACAD TIME	# OF SIM	SIM TIME	# OF FLTS	FLT TIME	PREREQUISITE	NOTES	CHAINING	EVENT CONV
DESG	6200	2LM Designation	B,R	E	A	1	(N*)	*	0	0.0	0	0.0	1	3.0				
		TOTAL DESG STAGE							0	0.0	0	0.0	1	3.0				
		RQD TOTAL (6000 PHASE)							6	6.0	0	0.0	3	6.0				
		TOTAL 5000,6000 STAGES							6	6.0	0	0.0	6	15.0				
		TOTAL 2000,3000,4000,5000,6000 STAGES							6	6.0	0	0.0	17	39.0				

CHAPTER 5

LOADMASTER

CHAPTER 5

LOADMASTER

5.0   INDIVIDUAL TRAINING AND READINESS REQUIREMENTS. This T&R syllabus is based on specific goals and performance standards designed to ensure individual proficiency in Core, Mission, and Core Plus Skills. The goal of this chapter is to develop individual and unit war fighting capabilities.

5.1   TRAINING PROGRESSION MODEL. This model represents the recommended training progression for the average C-9B Loadmaster. Units should use the model as a guide to generate individual training plans.

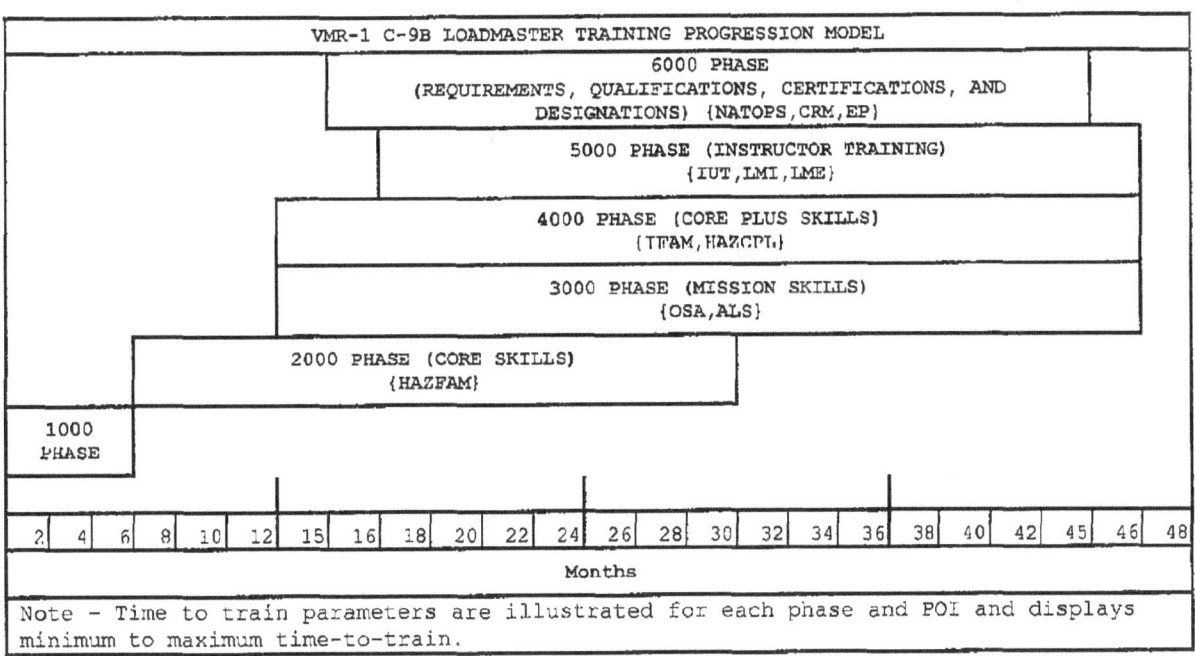

VMR-1 C-9B LOADMASTER TRAINING PROGRESSION MODEL

6000 PHASE
(REQUIREMENTS, QUALIFICATIONS, CERTIFICATIONS, AND DESIGNATIONS) {NATOPS,CRM,EP}

5000 PHASE (INSTRUCTOR TRAINING)
{IUT,LMI,LME}

4000 PHASE (CORE PLUS SKILLS)
{TFAM,HAZCPL}

3000 PHASE (MISSION SKILLS)
{OSA,ALS}

2000 PHASE (CORE SKILLS)
{HAZFAM}

1000 PHASE

2	4	6	8	10	12	15	16	18	20	22	24	26	28	30	32	34	36	38	40	42	45	46	48

Months

Note – Time to train parameters are illustrated for each phase and POI and displays minimum to maximum time-to-train.

5.2   ABBREVIATIONS

VMR-1 C-9B LOADMASTER	
CORE/MISSION/CORE PLUS SKILL ABBREVIATIONS	
CORE SKILLS (2000 Phase)	
FAM	Familiarization
CPL	Cargo and Passenger Loading
VFAM	VIP Familiarization
HAZFAM	Hazardous Cargo
LMUI	Loadmaster Under Instruction
MISSION SKILLS (3000 Phase)	
OSA	Operational Airlift Support
ALS	Air Logistics Support
CORE PLUS SKILLS (4000 Phase)	
IFAM	International/Transoceanic Familiarization
MAXCPL	Maximum Cargo
INSTRUCTOR (5000 Phase)	
LM ANI	Loadmaster Assistant NATOPS Instructor
LM NE/NI	Loadmaster NATOPS Evaluator / NATOPS Instructor
QUALIFICATIONS AND DESIGNATIONS (6000 Phase)	
ACAD	Academics
NTPS	NATOPS

| EP | Emergency Procedures |
| DESG | Designation |

5.3 DEFINITIONS

TERM	DEFINITION
Core Model	The Core Model is the basic foundation or standardized format by which all T&Rs are constructed. The Core Model provides the capability of quantifying both unit and individual training requirements and measuring readiness. This is accomplished by linking community Mission Statements, Mission Essential Task Lists, Output Standards, Core Skill Proficiency Requirements and Combat Leadership Matrices
Core Skill	Fundamental, environmental, or conditional capabilities required to perform basic functions. These basic functions serve as tactical enablers that allow crews to progress to the more complex Mission Skills. Primarily 2000 Phase events but may be introduced in the 1000 Phase.
Mission Skill	Mission Skills enable a unit to execute a specific MET. They are comprised of advanced event(s) that are focused on MET performance and draw upon the knowledge, aeronautical abilities, and situational awareness developed during Core Skill training. 3000 Phase events.
Core Plus Skill	Training events that can be theater specific or that have a low likelihood of occurrence. They may be fundamental, environmental, or conditional capabilities required to perform basic functions. 5000 Phase events.
Core Plus Mission	Training events that can be theater specific or that have a low likelihood of occurrence. They are comprised of advanced event(s) that are focused on Core Plus MET performance and draw upon the knowledge, aeronautical abilities, and situational awareness. 5000 Phase events.
Core Skill Proficiency (CSP)	CSP is a measure of training completion for 2000 Phase events. CSP is attained by executing all events listed in the Attain Table for each Core Skill. The individual must be simultaneously proficient in all events within that Core Skill to attain CSP.
Mission Skill Proficiency (MSP)	MSP is a measure of training completion for 3000 Phase events. MSP is attained by executing all events listed in the Attain Table for each Mission Skill. The individual must be simultaneously proficient in all events within that Mission Skill to attain MSP. MSP is directly related to Training Readiness.
Core Plus Skill Proficiency (CPSP)	CPSP is a measure of training completion for 5000 Phase "Skill" events. CPSP is attained by executing all events listed in the Attain Table for each Core Plus Skill. The individual must be simultaneously proficient in all events within that Core Plus Skill to attain CPSP
Core Plus Mission Proficiency (CPMP)	CPMP is a measure of training completion for 5000 Phase "Mission" events. CPMP is attained by executing all events listed in the Attain Table for each Core Plus Mission. The individual must be simultaneously proficient in all events within that Core Plus Mission to attain CPMP

5.4 INDIVIDUAL CORE/MISSION/CORE PLUS SKILL PROFICIENCY REQUIREMENTS

5.4.1 Management of individual CSP/MSP/CPSP/CPMP serves as the foundation for developing proficiency requirements in DRRS.

5.4.2 Individual CSP is a "Yes/No" status assigned to an individual by Core Skill. When an individual attains and maintains CSP in a Core Skill, the individual counts towards CMMR Unit CSP requirements for that Core Skill.

5.4.3 Proficiency is attained by individual Core/Mission/Core Plus skill and the training events to be executed within that skill set are determined by POI assignment (Basic, Transition, Conversion, Series Conversion, or Refresher).

5.4.4 Once proficiency has been attained by Core/Mission/Core Plus Skill (by any POI assignment) then the individual maintains proficiency by executing those events within the maintain column. An individual maintains proficiency by individual Core/Mission/Core Plus Skill.

Note
Individuals may be attaining proficiency
in some Core/Mission/Core Plus Skills
while maintaining proficiency in other
Core/Mission/Core Plus Skills.

5.4.5   Once proficiency has been attained, should one lose proficiency in an event in the maintain column, proficiency can be attained by demonstrating proficiency in the event which was delinquent. Should an individual lose proficiency in all events in the maintain column by Core/Mission/Core Plus Skill, the individual will be assigned to the Refresher POI for that Core/Mission/Core Plus Skill. To regain proficiency for that Core/Mission/Core Plus Skill the individual must demonstrate proficiency in all R-coded events for that Core/Mission/Core Plus Skill.

VMR-1 C-9B LOADMASTER						
CORE/MISSION/CORE PLUS ATTAIN & MAINTAIN MATRIX						
CORE SKILLS (2000 PHASE)						
STAGE	T&R CODE	ATTAIN PROFICIENCY				MAINTAIN PROFICIENCY
		BASIC POI		REFRESHER POI		MAINTAIN POI	
		STAGE	CODE	STAGE	CODE	STAGE	CODE
HAZFAM	2100R	HAZFAM	2100R	HAZFAM	2100R	HAZFAM	2100R
MISSION SKILLS (3000 PHASE)						
STAGE	T&R CODE	ATTAIN PROFICIENCY				MAINTAIN PROFICIENCY
		BASIC POI		REFRESHER POI		MAINTAIN POI	
		STAGE	CODE	STAGE	CODE	STAGE	CODE
OSA	3100R	OSA	3100R	OSA	3100R	OSA	3100R
ALS	3200R	ALS	3200R	ALS	3200R	ALS	3200R
CORE PLUS SKILLS (4000 PHASE)						
IFAM	4100	IFAM	4100	IFAM		IFAM	
IFAM	4101R		4101R		4101R		4101R
MAXCPL	4200	MAXCPL	4200	MAXCPL		MAXCPL	
MAXCPL	4201R		4201R		4201R		4201R
Note: An R suffix and Grey highlight = R-coded "Refresher" event						

5.5   CERTIFICATION, QUALIFICATION AND DESIGNATION TABLES. The tables below delineate T&R events required to be completed to attain proficiency, initial qualifications and designations. In addition to event requirements, all required stage lectures, briefs, squadron training, prerequisites, and other criteria shall be completed prior to completing final events. Certification, qualification and designation letters signed by the Commanding Officer shall be placed in Aircrew Performance Records (APR) and NATOPS. Loss of proficiency in all qualification events causes the associated qualification to be lost. Regaining a qualification requires completing all R-coded syllabus events associated with that qualification.

5.5.1 _ INSTRUCTOR DESIGNATIONS

VMR-1 C-9B LOADMASTER INSTRUCTOR DESIGNATIONS (5000 Phase)	
INSTRUCTOR DESIGNATION	EVENTS
LM ASSISTANT NATOPS INSTRUCTOR (LM ANI)	5100,5101
LM NATOPS INSTRUCTOR/NATOPS EVALUATOR (LM NI/NE)	5100,5101,5102

5.5.2   REQUIREMENTS, CERTIFICATIONS, QUALIFICATIONS, AND DESIGNATIONS

5.5.2.1 The table below delineates T&R events required to be completed to attain initial qualifications and designations. All stage lectures, briefs, squadron training, prerequisites, and open and closed book NATOPS exams shall be complete and graded prior to completing evaluation flights. Qualification and designation letters signed by the Commanding Officer shall be placed in individual NATOPS and APR jackets.

VMR-1 C-9B LOADMASTER	
REQUIREMENTS, CERTIFICATIONS, QUALIFICATIONS, AND DESIGNATIONS (R,C,Q,& D) [6000 Phase]	
QUALIFICATIONS	
NATOPS	6000,6001,6002,6100
CRM	6005,6101
DESIGNATIONS	
LM	6200

5.6   VMR-1 C-9B LOADMASTER PROGRAMS OF INSTRUCTION (POI). All Loadmaster training shall be performed in accordance with this T&R chapter, OPNAVINST 3710.7, current Squadron directives, and NAVAIR's 01-C9BAAA-1, 01-C9BAAA-9, 01-1B-50, and MCO P4030.19.

5.6.1   The time required to qualify a C-9B Loadmaster will vary depending on previous experience and flight time availability. All LMUIs shall have been previously designated as 2nd Loadmaster (2LM) in the C-9B. Training should be accomplished in conjunction with operational flights, however, it is acceptable to train aboard dedicated training missions through the use of self-built palletized cargo. Every effort should be made to conduct VIP training codes aboard actual VIP Code missions, however, it is permissible to conduct simulated VIP missions as required in order to continue student Loadmasters through the syllabus. Hazardous Cargo flights may also be simulated.

5.6.2   Basic/Conversion POI. A Basic Loadmaster shall be defined as a C-9B Loadmaster who obtains all Loadmaster training aboard the C-9B and was not previously qualified as a KC-130 Loadmaster/Crewmaster (MOS 7382,6276). A Conversion Loadmaster shall be defined as a C-9B Loadmaster who was previously qualified as a KC-130 Loadmaster/Crewmaster. Both Basic and Conversion Loadmasters shall be qualified as C-9B 2nd Loadmasters and fly 100 hours (waiverable by the Commanding Officer), as C-9B 2LM prior to commencing this POI. The LM/LMI shall be screened by the squadron Aircrew Screening Board and approved by the Commanding Officer prior to commencing this POI. All decisions as to POI eligibility rest with the Commanding Officer. The LM Under Instruction (LMUI) shall be considered qualified to function as a qualified LM on CONUS missions and passenger and cargo missions upon completion of the LM designation flight (DESG-6200). Upon completion of the LM designation, the LM must complete OSA-3100 and ALS-3200 under the supervision of an instructor prior to performing those duties individually. The International/Transoceanic flights (IFAM 4100 and IFAM 4101) are established to ensure the LM has been exposed to overwater/international procedures prior to assignment to the LM Instructor and LM NATOPS Instructor/Evaluator Phases. As such, these flights shall be complete prior to commencing the LM Instructor or LM NATOPS instructor/evaluator syllabus.

5.6.2.1 A Basic Loadmaster shall be considered qualified to serve as the Loadmaster aboard both CONUS and OCONUS missions.

5.6.2.2 The Loadmaster must be complete with MAXCPL 2500-2501 prior to acting as the Loadmaster aboard missions carrying maximum cargo (SECOs E, G, or H).

VMR-1 C-9B LOADMASTER Basic POI		
Weeks	Phase of Instruction	Unit
1	Water survival/flight physiology	NAWSTP
3	Ground training	VMR-1
1	Loadmaster course	CLFSW, Fort Worth JRB
2	Core Skill Introduction (1000 Phase)	VMR-1
3	Core Skill (2000 Phase)	VMR-1
1	Mission Skill (3000 Phase)	VMR-1
2	Core Plus Skills (4000 Phase)	VMR-1

5.6.3   Refresher POI. A Refresher Loadmaster shall be defined as a previously designated C-9B Loadmaster who has been assigned to other duty preventing currency in the C-9B aircraft for a period exceeding 12 months. A Loadmaster who has been assigned to other duty preventing currency in the C-9B aircraft for a period exceeding 12 months is not eligible for Refresher Loadmaster training and must complete the Basic POI. The LMUI shall have been recommended by the squadron Standardization Board and approved by the Commanding Officer prior to commencing this Refresher POI. All decisions as to POI eligibility rest with the Commanding Officer.

VMR-1 C-9B LOADMASTER Refresher POI		
Weeks	Phase of Instruction	Unit
1	Water survival/flight physiology *	NAWSTP
3	Core Introduction (1000 Phase)	VMR-1
4	Core Skill (2000 Phase)	VMR-1
2	Mission Skill (3000 Phase)	VMR-1
2	Core Plus Skills (4000 Phase)	VMR-1
*Required only if NAWSTP swim qualification is expired.		

5.6.5   POI FOR INSTRUCTOR LOADMASTER UNDER TRAINING (IUT). The Loadmaster Instructor qualification is reserved for those Loadmasters that demonstrate the maturity, knowledge, and instructional ability to successfully complete the training. The LMIUT shall have been recommended by the squadron Standardization Board and approved by the Commanding Officer prior to commencing this POI. All decisions as to POI eligibility rest with the Commanding Officer. The LMIUT will complete IFAM-4100 and IFAM-4101 prior to assignment to the 2LM Instructor or 2LM NATOPS Instructor/Evaluator Training.

VMR-1 C-9B LOADMASTER Instructor POI		
Weeks	Phase of Instruction	Unit
1	LM Instructor Training	VMR-1
2	LM NATOPS Evaluator Training	VMR-1

5.7   SYLLABUS NOTES

5.7.1   Environmental Conditions Matrix

Environmental Conditions	
Code	Meaning
D	Shall be flown during hours of daylight: (by exception - there is no use of a symbol)
N*	Shall be flown during hours of darkness must be flown unaided
(N*)	May be flown during hours of darkness - If flown during hours of darkness must be flown unaided
Note - If the event is to be flown in the simulator the Simulator Instructor shall set the desired environmental conditions for the event.	

5.7.2   Device Matrix

DEVICE (Aviation Flying)	
Symbol	Meaning
A	Flown in aircraft
A/S	Aircraft preferred may be flown in simulator
S	Flown in simulator
S/A	Simulator preferred may be flown in aircraft
Note – If the event is to be flown in the simulator the Simulator Instructor shall set the desired environmental conditions for the event.	

5.7.3   Program of Instruction Matrix

PROGRAM OF INSTRUCTION MATRIX			
Program of Instruction (POI)	Symbol	Aviation Flying	Aviation Ground
Basic	B	Initial MOS/Skill Training	Initial MOS training
Refresher	R	DIFDEN to DIFOPS in same T/M/S	Return to community from non (MOS/Skill) associated tour
Maintain	M	All individuals who have attained CSP/MSP/CPP by initial POI assignment are re-assigned to the M POI to maintain proficiency.	

5.7.5   Event Terms

EVENT TERMS	
TERM	DESCRRIPTION
Discuss	An explanation of systems, procedures, or maneuvers during the brief, in flight, or post flight. Student is responsible for knowledge of procedures.
Demonstrate	The description and performance of a particular maneuver/event by the instructor, observed by the LMUI/student. The LMUI/student is responsible for knowledge of the procedures prior to the demonstration of a required maneuver/student.
Introduce	The instructor may demonstrate a procedure or maneuver to a student, or may coach the LMUI through the maneuver without demonstration. The LMUI performs the procedures or maneuver with coaching as necessary. The LMUI is responsible for knowledge of the procedures.
Practice	The performance of a maneuver or procedure by the LMUI/student that may have been previously introduced in order to attain a specified level of performance.
Review	Demonstrated proficiency of a maneuver by the LMUI/student.
Evaluate	Any flight designed to evaluate aircrew standardization that does not fit another category such as SARCK, HACCK, T2PCK, etc.
E-Coded	This term means that documentation (ATF) is required each time the event is logged. Requires evaluation by a certified standardization instructor (NATOPS I, WTI, INST Evaluator etc.)

5.8   CORE SKILL INTRODUCTION FRS ACADEMIC PHASE (0000 Phase). There are no 0000 Phase events in the C-9B T&R manual. However, the squadron training listed below is required.

5.8.1   The following ground training syllabus is intended as squadron-level training for Basic Loadmaster Students during initial qualification. Refresher Loadmasters are exempt from this ground training syllabus.

5.8.2   The Loadmaster student may commence this ground training syllabus either before or after attending the C-9B Loadmaster Course at Fort Worth JRB. This ground training may be conducted concurrently with the flight training syllabus. Additionally, the Loadmaster student is permitted to commence the flight training syllabus prior to attending the Loadmaster Course at Fort Worth JRB. However, the ground training syllabus and the Loadmaster Course at Fort Worth JRB must be complete prior to the DESG-6200 flight. The Commanding Officer may waive the C-9B Loadmaster course for Conversion Loadmasters only.

Week 1

    (1) General aircraft description
    (2) Aircraft systems
    (3) Aircraft emergency equipment and systems
    (4) Emergency procedures
    (5) Loadmaster equipment
    (6) Weight and balance theory and formulas
    (7) Weight and balance forms (DD Form 365)
    (8) Aircraft limitations passenger/cargo manifests
    (9) Associated paperwork
    (10) Weight and balance form computation utilizing moment
    (11) Procedures for arranging crew billeting and ground transportation

Week 2

    (1) Cargo restraint equipment
    (2) Weight and balance planning
    (3) Personal flying equipment requirements
    (4) Phase examinations
    (5) Cargo limitations and dimensions
    (6) Dimensions of main cabin area
    (7) Dimensions of cargo doors
    (8) Dimensions of cargo compartments
    (9) Weight restrictions for decking and pallets
    (10) Loadmaster equipment and responsibilities listed in NATOPS manual
    (11) Written exam on material in the Cargo Loading Manual
       (NAVAIR 1-C9BAAA-9-9)

Week 3

    (1) C-9 configurations
    (2) Loadex 1 SECO C
    (3) Loadex 2 SECO G
    (4) Loadex 3 special aircraft configurations
    (5) Aircraft mission
    (6) Preflight coordination with Lift Coordinator
    (7) Crew billeting and ground transportation requirements
    (8) NATOPS open and closed book examinations

5.9   CORE SKILL INTRODUCTION PHASE (1000). The Core Skill Introduction Phase is designed to familiarize the LMUI with C-9B normal procedures, CRM, cargo and passenger loading, and emergency procedures.

5.10   CORE SKILL INTRODUCTION STAGES (1000)

PARAGRAPH	STAGE
5.10.1	Familiarization (FAM)
5.10.2	Cargo and Passenger Loading (CPL)
5.10.3	Distinguished Passengers (VIP)

5.10.1   Familiarization Flights (FAM)

5.10.1.1 Purpose. Familiarize the LMUI with the C-9B aircraft and procedures required of a qualified LM during all emergencies.

5.10.1.2 Crew Requirements. TAC, T2P, CC, LMI, LMUI, 2LM

FAM-1000   2.0   *   B,R   (N*)   A   1 C-9B

    Goal. Introduce the LMUI to the responses/action required during each airborne/ground emergency.

Requirement

Discuss/Demonstrate/Introduce

Rapid depressurization/emergency descent
Fuselage fire
Cabin smoke/fume elimination
In-flight hazardous spill
Crash landing/abnormal landing/ditching procedures
Demonstrate the use/refilling of walk around oxygen bottles
Use/location of all emergency equipment
"Don" the restraining harness and demonstrate the procedure for
  securing the restraining harness

Review

Ground training material

Performance Standard. LMUI will demonstrate proficiency in all previously covered training and have a general knowledge of all items covered pertaining to FAM-1000.

Prerequisite. Designated 2LM on the C-9B

5.10.2 Cargo and Passenger Loading (CPL)

5.10.2.1 Purpose. Instruct and qualify the LMUI in the performance of the duties required to load cargo and passengers. Emphasize adherence to NATOPS procedures, operation of aircraft equipment and all duties and procedures required of a qualified C-9B Loadmaster.

5.10.2.2 Crew Requirements. TAC, T2P, CC, LMI, LMUI, 2LM

| CPL-1100 | 2.0 | * | B | | (N*) | | A | 1 C-9B |

Goal. Introduce the LMUI to passenger/baggage loading procedures and weight and balance form computation. Additionally, the LMUI will be instructed on the proper pre-flight and post flight procedures.

Requirement

Discuss/Demonstrate/Introduce

LMUI observes and assists a qualified LM during pre-flight, post flight, and passenger/baggage loading and offloading, to include the directing of ground loading equipment around the aircraft. LMUI will compute a secondary weight and balance form. Emphasis will be on pre-flight of aircraft, in-flight responsibilities and aircraft post flight. The LMI will introduce the procedures for pre-flight coordination with the Lift Coordinator.

Performance Standard. LMUI will demonstrate proficiency in all previously covered training and have a general knowledge of all items covered pertaining to CPL-1100.

Prerequisite. FAM-1000.

| CPL-1101 | 3.0 | * | B,R | | (N*) | | A | 1 C-9B |

Goal. Continuation of passenger and baggage loading procedures and Weight and Balance Form computation.

Requirement

Discuss/Demonstrate/Introduce

The LMUI will demonstrate a thorough knowledge of the aircraft lighting systems and lavatory and galley operation, to include restrictions and circuit breaker locations. Additionally, LMUI will demonstrate knowledge of meal handling procedures.

Review

The LMUI must complete the primary weight and balance form, prior to scheduled take-off, on a flight consisting of an enroute stop emphasizing accurate passenger manifests, weight and balance form, associated paperwork, pre-flight, in-flight and post flight responsibilities.

Performance Standard. LMUI will demonstrate proficiency in all previously covered training and have a general knowledge of all items covered pertaining to CPL-1101.

Prerequisite. CPL-1100

CPL-1102   3.0   *   B,R   (N*)   A   1 C-9B

Goal. The LMUI will perform all duties of C-9B Loadmaster.

Requirement

Discuss/Demonstrate/Introduce

The LMUI will demonstrate a thorough knowledge of the aircraft lighting systems and lavatory and galley operation, to include restrictions and circuit breaker locations.

Review

The LMUI must complete the primary weight and balance form, prior to scheduled take-off, on a flight consisting of an enroute stop emphasizing accurate passenger manifests, weight and balance form, associated paperwork, pre-flight, in-flight and post flight responsibilities, and meal handling procedures.

Performance Standard. LMUI will demonstrate proficiency in all previously covered training and have a general knowledge of all items covered pertaining to CPL-1102.

Prerequisite. CPL-1101

CPL-1103   3.0   *   B,R   (N*)   A   1 C-9B

Goal. LMUI observes and assists a qualified Loadmaster during flight with mixed cargo and passengers.

Requirement

Discuss/Demonstrate/Introduce

Flight will consist of an enroute stops emphasizing "SECO C" and "SECO G" configuration. The LMUI will demonstrate a thorough knowledge of the operation of the cargo door, cargo door restrictions, and associated hydraulic systems (to include circuit breaker locations). Additionally, the LMUI will properly install the door sills and compute a secondary weight and balance form.

Performance Standard. LMUI will demonstrate proficiency in all previously covered training and have a general knowledge of all items covered pertaining to CPL-1103.

Prerequisite. CPL-1102

CPL-1104   3.0   *   B   (N*)   A   1 C-9B

Goal. LMUI observes and assists a qualified loadmaster during flight with mixed cargo and passengers.

Requirement

Discuss/Demonstrate/Introduce

Flight will consist of an enroute stop emphasizing aircraft

dimensions, compartment weight restrictions, and restraint criteria. The LMUI will be instructed in the expeditious off-load of baggage. Additionally, the LMUI will observe and assist with the staging and proper loading of cargo, the use of tie down equipment, and manifests.

Performance Standard. LMUI will demonstrate proficiency in all previously covered training and have a general knowledge of all items covered pertaining to CPL-1104. The LMUI will complete a secondary Weight and Balance Form prior to departure.

Prerequisite. CPL-1103

CPL-1105   3.0   *   B,R   (N*)   A   1 C-9B

Goal. The LMUI will observe and assist a qualified Loadmaster during the loading and the unloading of palletized cargo.

Requirement

Discuss/Demonstrate/Introduce

Flight will consist of an enroute stop. Emphasis will be placed on the procedures for loading and unloading palletized cargo. The use of established loading signals will be utilized during all loading and unloading evolutions.

Review

The LMUI will compute the primary weight and balance form and will determine the required tie down restraint. Safety of aircraft and personnel will be the primary consideration.

Performance Standard. LMUI will demonstrate proficiency in all previously covered training and have a general knowledge of all items covered pertaining to CPL-1105. The LMUI will complete a secondary weight and balance form prior to departure.

Prerequisite. CPL-1104

CPL-1106   2.0   *   B   (N*)   A   1 C-9B

Goal. Review CPL-1100 through CPL-1105.

Requirement

Discuss/Review

Flight will consist of an overnight stop. Emphasis will be placed upon review of operation of the cargo door, cargo door restrictions, and associated hydraulic systems. The LMUI will demonstrate the loading of baggage and will compute the primary weight and balance form. Additionally, LMUI will demonstrate knowledge of the process of arranging billeting and transportation for the crew from the aircraft to billeting and return the next morning.

Performance Standard. LMUI will demonstrate proficiency in all previously covered training.

Prerequisite. CPL-1105

CPL-1107   3.0   *   B,R   (N*)   A   1 C-9B

Goal. Progress review. LMUI performs all duties required of a C-9B Loadmaster.

Requirement

Review

Flight will consist of an enroute stop. Emphasis will be placed on weight and balance form computation (prior to scheduled take-off), appropriate tie down procedures, required tie down restraint, and safety in the use of all loading equipment. The LUI will be observed/evaluated on the directing of forklift operators and ground loading equipment around the aircraft.

Performance Standard. LMUI will demonstrate proficiency in all previously covered LM training.

Prerequisite. CPL-1105

5.10.3 Distinguished Passengers (VIP)

5.10.3.1 Purpose. Qualify a LMUI in the proper procedures when carrying passengers who are VIP Code 7 or above.

5.10.3.2 Crew Requirements. TAC, T2P, CC, LMI, LMUI, 2LM

VFAM-1200   2.0   *   B   (N*)   A   1 C-9B

Goal. The LMUI will observe a qualified Loadmaster on a flight carrying a passenger that is VIP Code 7 or above.

Requirement

Discuss/Demonstrate

Emphasis will be placed on passenger comfort, VIP baggage handling, aircraft configuration, and the installation of the appropriate VIP placard. Weight and balance form computation will be accomplished by the Loadmaster Instructor (LMI).

Performance Standard. LMUI will demonstrate proficiency in all previously covered training and have a general knowledge of all items covered pertaining to VFAM-1200.

Prerequisite. FAM-1000. However this code may be flown simultaneously with a FAM-1000 if the first training opportunity consists of a VIP mission.

VFAM-1201   2.0   *   B,R   (N*)   A   1 C-9B

Goal. Progress review.

Requirement

Review

The LMUI will perform all Loadmaster duties on a flight carrying a VIP Code 7 or above. Emphasis will be placed on passenger comfort, VIP baggage handling, aircraft preparation, and an accurate weight and balance form.

Performance Standard. LMUI will demonstrate proficiency in all previously covered training and be proficient in conducting Loadmaster VIP procedures.

Prerequisite. VFAM-1200

5.11 CORE SKILL PHASE (2000)

5.11.1 General

Core Skill Phase in the C-9B introduces the LMUI to the requirements and responsibilities when carrying hazardous materials.

5.12   CORE SKILL INTRODUCTION STAGES (2000)

PARAGRAPH	STAGE
5.12.1	Hazardous Cargo (HAZFAM)

5.12.1   Hazardous Cargo (HAZFAM)

5.12.1.1 Purpose. Familiarize and qualify the LMUI in the proper procedures when carrying hazardous cargo.

5.12.1.2 Crew Requirements. TAC, T2P, CC, LME, LMUI, 2LM

HAZFAM-2100 2.0   1095 B,R,M   (N*)   A   1 C-9B

> Goal. To give an LMUI the required training that is needed to properly read and identify all information on a shippers declaration of hazardous goods form and be able to find all applicable information on that form in the MCO P4030.19 Hazardous Material Manual.
>
> Requirement
>
> > Discuss/Demonstrate/Introduce/Review
> >
> > > Emphasize total compliance with MCO P4030.19 to include all required forms, any deviations and/or waivers, and Pilot In Command required brietings. The LMUI will compute the weight and balance form and will also complete and file all flight related paperwork.
>
> Performance Standard. LMUI will demonstrate proficiency in all previously covered training and have a general knowledge of all items covered pertaining to HAZFAM-2400.
>
> Prerequisite. FAM-1000, Completion of Loadmaster School at Fort Worth JRB.

5.13   MISSION SKILLS PHASE (3000)

5.13.1   General. The Mission Skill Phase is designed to familiarize the LMUI with the unique missions and challenges associated with the VMR-1, C-9B. Mission Skills are designed to fulfill the requirements of the C-9B Mission Essential Task List as defined by the associated Marine Corps Task (MCT).

5.14   MISSION SKILL STAGES (3000)

PARAGRAPH	STAGE
5.14.1	Operational Support Airlift (OSA)
5.14.2	Air Logistics Support (ALS)

5.14.1   Operational Support Airlift (OSA)

5.14.1.1 Purpose. This event is designed to fulfill the requirement set in MCT 1.3.5.1.2, conduct OSA.

5.14.1.2 General. It is understood that many missions will be a combination of both passenger and cargo transportation and both codes will be used when filling out the NAVFLIR. Both codes are made available for flights that clearly fall into a single category.

5.14.1.3 Crew Requirement. Full mission crew.

OSA-3100   6.0   180   B,R,M   (N*)   A   1 C-9B

> Goal. Introduce the LMUI to the JOSAC/ASM passenger mission or provide continued update to the skills of the LM while performing the passenger mission.
>
> Requirement
> Execute a safe and successful passenger mission to include completion of required paper work.
>
> Performance Standard. LM/LMUI will execute a safe and successful passenger mission to include accurate completion of all required paper work.
>
> Prerequisite. DESG-6200

5.14.2 Air Logistics Support (ALS)

5.14.2.1 Purpose. This event is designed to fulfill the requirement set in MMC 5.3.8, conduct ALS.

5.14.2.2 General. It is understood that many missions will be a combination of both passenger and cargo transportation and both codes will be used when filling out the NAVFLIR. Both codes are made available for flights that clearly fall into a single category.

5.14.2.3 Crew Requirement. Full mission crew.

ALS-3200   2.0   180   B,R,M   (N*)   A   1 C-9B

> Goal. Introduce the LMUI to the C-9B cargo mission or provide continued update to the skills used while performing the cargo mission.
>
> Requirement. Execute a safe and successful cargo mission to include completion of required paper work.
>
> Performance Standard. LM/LMUI will execute a safe and successful cargo mission to include accurate completion of all required paper work.
>
> Prerequisite. DESG-6200

5.15 CORE PLUS SKILL PHASE (4000)

5.15.1 General. Core Skill Plus Phase in the C-9B introduces the LMUI to the requirements and responsibilities when flying internationally and carrying maximum cargo loads.

5.16 CORE PLUS SKILL INTRODUCTION STAGES (4000)

PARAGRAPH	STAGE
5.16.1	International/Trans Oceanic Flights (IFAM)
5.16.2	Max Load Introduction (MAXCPL)

5.16.1 International/Trans Oceanic Flights (IFAM)

5.16.1.1 Purpose. Qualify the Loadmaster in overwater/international procedures with cargo and/or passengers aboard the aircraft.

5.16.1.2 Crew Requirements. TAC, T2P, CC, LMI, LMUI, 2LM

IFAM-4100   3.0   *   B   (N*)   A   1 C-9B

> Goal. The LMUI observes and assists a LMI during an international/ trans oceanic flight with passengers and/or cargo aboard.

Requirement

Discuss/Demonstrate/Introduce

The LMUI will observe and assist the LMI during pre-flight, in-flight, and post-flight duties. Emphasis will be placed on maximum passenger loads for international/trans oceanic flight, proper baggage handling, accurate passenger manifests, weight and balance form, required customs and agriculture procedures, appropriate emergency equipment and required briefings. Additionally, LMUI will assist LMI in arranging billeting and ground transportation for an OCONUS location.

Review

Previously covered material as necessary

Performance Standard. LUMI will demonstrate proficiency in all previously covered training and have a general knowledge of all items covered pertaining to IFAM 2300.

Prerequisite. FAM-1000

IFAM-4101   3.0   365   B,R,M   (N*)   A   1 C-9B

Goal. The LMUI will perform all duties required of a Loadmaster on an overwater flight with passengers and/or cargo aboard while under the supervision of a Loadmaster Instructor. Qualified LMs will use this code to update currency.

Requirement

Review

The LMUI will maintain accurate weight and balance form, customs/agriculture inspection documents, passenger manifests and leg load information. The LMUI will conduct the appropriate pre-flight, in-flight and post flight duties.

Performance Standard. LMUI will demonstrate proficiency in all Loadmaster international/trans oceanic flight procedures with minimal instructor supervision. Qualified Loadmasters will execute an OCONUS flight safely and proficiently.

Prerequisite. IFAM-4100

5.16.2   Maximum Cargo Procedures (MAXCPL)

5.16.2.1 Purpose. Qualify the LMUI in maximum cargo procedures (SECOs E, F or H).

5.16.2.2 Crew Requirements. TAC, T2P, CC, LME, LMUI, 2LM

MAXCPL-4200 3.0   *   B   (N*)   A   1 C-9B

Goal. The LMUI will observe and assist a Loadmaster NATOPS Instructor/Evaluator on a flight carrying maximum cargo, (SECO's E, G or H).

Requirement

Discuss/Demonstrate/Introduce

Emphasize the reconfiguration of the aircraft to SECO E, F or H. The LMUI will compute the primary weight and balance form. The loading of the aircraft must be accomplished to allow the minimum amount of interference at intermediate stops with due consideration to center of gravity limits. The LMUI will ensure the cargo is properly restrained to the pallet and that no pallet exceeds the appropriate "G" factor limitation. The LMUI will install the "barrier net.".

Performance Standard. LMUI will demonstrate an understanding of all max cargo Loadmaster related duties.

Prerequisite. CPL-1104

MAXCPL-4201 3.0   1095 B,R,M   (N*)   A   1 C-9B

   Goal. The LMUI will perform all Loadmaster duties on a flight carrying maximum cargo, (SECO's E, G, or H) under the supervision of a Loadmaster NATOPS Instructor/Evaluator.

   Requirement

      Review

         Emphasize reconfiguration of the aircraft to the required SECO configuration. The correct placement of all pallet restraints will be verified by the LMUI. The LMUI will compute the weight and balance form with consideration to enroute stops and center of gravity limitations. The LMUI will stage all cargo and load the aircraft with the safety of the aircraft, the safety of loading personnel, and control of all loading equipment as the primary consideration.

   Performance Standard. LMUI will demonstrate proficiency in all Max cargo loadmaster related duties.

Prerequisite. MAXCPL-4200

5.17   INSTRUCTOR TRAINING PHASE (5000)

5.17.1 General. The instructor training phase is designed to provide the Squadron with a cadre of qualified instructors needed to ensure quality training at all times.

PARAGRAPH	STAGE
5.18.1	Instructor Under Training (IUT)

5.17.2 Instructor under Training (IUT)

5.17.2.1 Purpose. Develop qualified instructor Loadmasters with the ability to teach all phases of C-9B flight and mission requirements.

5.17.2.2 General. A LMI is qualified to instruct in all phases of aircraft operations. Also, a LM must have 100 hours in the C-9B (waiverable by the Commanding Officer), before being recommended for the instructor syllabus.

5.17.2.2 Crew Requirements. TAC, T2P, CC, LM NE/NI, LMIUI, LMUI, 2LM

IUT-5100   2.0   *   B,R   E   (N*) A   1 C-9B

   Goal. Instruction introduction.

   Requirement

      Discuss

         Conduct a fight, and all LM ground/flight responsibilities and how they are taught to a LMUI.

      Review

         The LMIUT will perform all duties of a LMI on a flight with a LMUI while being evaluated by a LM NATOPS Instructor (NI).

Review T&R and syllabus evaluation forms.

Performance Standard. LMIUT should have a solid knowledge of aircraft and LM responsibilities during all aspects of ground and flight operations.

Prerequisite. 6200

IUT-5101   2.0   *   B,R   E   (N*)   A   1 C-9B

Goal. Qualify the LM as a LM ANI.

Requirement

Discuss

Conduct of evaluation flight
Review all LM/LMI ground and flight responsibilities, publications, and required documentation.

Review

The LMIUT shall be evaluated by a LM NATOPS Instructor/Evaluator while instructing a LMUI. The LMIUT being evaluated must display the maturity, integrity, and knowledge of the aircraft required to conduct a NATOPS evaluation.

Performance Standard. LMIUT will demonstrate the requisite maturity, instructional ability, and standardization expected of an LM ANI.

Prerequisite. IUT-5100

IUT-5102   3.0   *   B,R   (N*)   E   A   1 C-9B

Goal. Qualify the LMI as a NATOPS Instructor/Evaluator.

Requirement

Discuss

Conduct of evaluation flight
Responsibilities of the 2LM NI/NE

Review

The 2LMI shall be evaluated by a 2LM NATOPS Instructor/ Evaluator while instructing a 2LMUI. The LM being evaluated must display the maturity, integrity, and knowledge of the aircraft required to conduct a NATOPS evaluation.

Performance Standard. Student will demonstrate the requisite maturity, instructional ability, and standardization expected of a LM NI/NE.

Prerequisite. IUT-5101

5.18   REQUIREMENTS, CERTIFICATIONS, QUALIFICATIONS, AND DESIGNATIONS (RCQD) PHASE (6000)

5.18.1   General. The 6000 phase encompasses the events required to maintain currency with all certifications, qualifications, and designations.

5.19   REQUIREMENTS, CERTIFICATIONS, QUALIFICATIONS, AND DESIGNATIONS (RCQD) STAGES (6000)

PARAGRAPH	STAGE
5.21.1	Academics (ACAD)
5.21.2	NATOPS Evaluations (NTPS)
5.21.3	Designations (DESG)

5.19.1 Academics (ACAD)

5.19.1.1 Purpose. To complete the academic requirements for subsequent annual evaluation flights.

ACAD-6000   1.0   365   B,R,M   E

   Goal. The NATOPS open book examination shall consist of, but not be limited to the question bank. The purpose of the open book examination is to evaluate the Loadmaster's knowledge of the appropriate publications and the aircraft.

   Performance Standard. Achieve a minimum score of 3.5 on the open book examination.

ACAD-6001   1.0   365   B,R,M   E

   Goal. The purpose of the NATOPS closed book examination is to evaluate the Loadmaster's knowledge of the concerning normal/emergency procedures and aircraft limitations.

   Performance Standard. Achieve a minimum score of 3.3 on the closed book examination (NATOPS standard).
   Prerequisite. ACAD-6000

ACAD-6002   1.0   365   B,R,M   E

   Goal. The NATOPS oral examination shall consist of, but not be limited to the question bank. The instructor may draw upon their experience to propose questions of a direct and positive manner and in no way be opinionated to evaluate the Loadmaster's knowledge of the concerning normal/emergency procedures, aircraft limitations, and performance.

   Performance Standard. Achieve a minimum grade of qualified on the oral examination.

   Prerequisite. ACAD-6000 and ACAD-6001

ACAD-6005   1.0   365   B,R,M   E

   Goal. CRM ground instruction in accordance with applicable directives and instructions.

   Performance Standard. Demonstrate satisfactory knowledge of CRM principles and their application.

ACAD-6006   1.0   30   B,R,M   E

   Goal. Monthly emergency procedures exam.

   Requirement. Conduct a monthly emergency procedures exam per NAVMC 3500.15.

ACAD-6007   1.0   90   B,R,M   (N)   E   S/A   1 C-9B

   Goal. Emergency Procedure Review.

   Requirement. This event will review C-9B emergency procedures and fulfills the requirement of quarterly emergency procedures simulator training per NAVMC 3500.14. This event can be accomplished in the aircraft while airborne or on the deck.

   Performance Standard. Comply with C-9B NFM emergency procedures.

5.19.2   NATOPS Evaluations (NTPS)

5.19.2.1 Purpose.   Provide annual NATOPS and CRM evaluation flights.

NTPS-6100   3.0   365   B,R,M   (N)   E   A/S   1 C-9B

    Goal.   Conduct annual NATOPS evaluation.

    Requirement.   Proficiency in the utilization of all aspects of the C-9B.   The proficiency expected by the evaluator in this flight shall be commensurate with the experience of the Loadmaster under evaluation.

    Performance Standard.   The performance expected by the evaluator in this flight shall be commensurate with the experience level of the Loadmaster under evaluation.

    Prerequisite.   ACAD-6000, ACAD-6001, and ACAD-6002 within 60 days preceding this event.   DESG-6200.

NTPS-6101   3.0   365   B,R,M   (N)   E   A/S   1 C-9B

    Goal.   Conduct annual CRM evaluation.

    Requirement.   Perform initial/annual CRM flight evaluation per applicable directives.   May be flown in conjunction with annual NATOPS evaluation flight.

    Performance Standard.   Performance standards will be according to the C-9B NFM.

    Prerequisite.   ACAD-6005

5.19.3   Designation Flights (DESG)

5.19.3.1 Purpose.   To provide an evaluation flight for designation as a LM.

5.19.3.2 General.   LMUI will successfully complete a flight evaluation administered by a designated NATOPS Loadmaster Instructor.

DESG-6200   3.0   *   B,R   (N*)   E   A   1 C-9B

    Goal.   LMUI evaluation flight.   LMUI to demonstrate the ability to meet NATOPS qualification per Chapter 18 NATOPS evaluation criteria.   The flight evaluation is designed to measure with maximum objectivity the degree of standardization demonstrated by the LMUI and to ensure safety of flight.

    Requirement

        Brief/Discuss

            The LMUI should be prepared to brief/discuss all previously introduced material.

        Review

            All previously introduced training shall be covered with particular attention given to NATOPS and emergency procedures.

    Performance Standard.   The LMUI Check should emphasize only those areas that are germane to the Loadmaster duties and demonstrated performance required to safely execute these duties.

    Prerequisite.   ACAD-6000, ACAD-6001, and ACAD-6002 within 60 days preceding this event.   1000 and 2000 series complete.   Ground School complete, Loadmaster School complete.

5.20   T&R ATTAIN AND MAINTAIN SYLLABUS MATRICES

VMR-1 C-9B
LOADMASTER
CORE/MISSION/CORE PLUS ATTAIN & MAINTAIN MATRIX

CORE SKILLS (2000 PHASE)

T&R EVENT INFORMATION				ATTAIN PROFICIENCY				MAINTAIN PROFICIENCY			
				BASIC POI		REFRESHER POI		MAINTAIN POI			
T&R DESCRIPTION	STAGE	CODE	RE FLY	STAGE	CODE	STAGE	CODE	STAGE	CODE	PREREQUISITES	CHAINING
Hazardous Materials	HAZFAM	2400R	1095	HAZFAM	2400R	HAZFAM	2400R	HAZFAM	2400R		

MISSION SKILLS (3000 PHASE)

T&R EVENT INFORMATION				ATTAIN PROFICIENCY				MAINTAIN PROFICIENCY			
				BASIC POI		REFRESHER POI		MAINTAIN POI			
T&R DESCRIPTION	STAGE	CODE	RE FLY	STAGE	CODE	STAGE	CODE	STAGE	CODE	PREREQUISITES	CHAINING
Passenger Mission	OSA	3100R	180	OSA	3100R	OSA	3100R	OSA	3100R	6200	3200
Cargo Mission	ALS	3200R	180	ALS	3200R	ALS	3200R	ALS	3200R	6200	3100

CORE PLUS SKILLS (4000 PHASE)

T&R EVENT INFORMATION				ATTAIN PROFICIENCY				MAINTAIN PROFICIENCY			
				BASIC POI		REFRESHER POI		MAINTAIN POI			
T&R DESCRIPTION	STAGE	CODE	RE FLY	STAGE	CODE	STAGE	CODE	STAGE	CODE	PREREQUISITES	CHAINING
Int/Trans O Intro	IFAM	4100	*	IFAM	2300	IFAM	2302R	IFAM	2301R	4100	
Int/Trans O Review	IFAM	4101R	365		2301R						
Max Load Introduction	MAXCPL	4200	*	MAXCPL	4200	MAXCPL				4200	
Max Load Rev	MAXCPL	4201R	1095		4201R		4201R		4201R		

Enclosure (1)

5.21   T&R SYLLABUS MATRIX

VMR-1 LOADMASTER T&R MATRIX

STAGE	TRNG CODE	T&R DESCRIPTION	POI	E DEVICE	# OF A/C	CON	RE FLY	# OF ACAD	ACAD TIME	# OF SIM	SIM TIME	# OF FLTS	FLT TIME	PREREQUISITE	NOTES	CHAINING	EVENT CONV
		CORE SKILL INTRODUCTION TRAINING (1000 PHASE EVENTS)															
		FAMILIARIZATION (FAM)															
FAM	1000	Emergency Procedures	B,R	A	1	(N*)	*	0	0.0	0	0.0	1	2.0	2LM Designation			
		TOTAL FAM STAGE						0	0.0	0	0.0	1	2.0				
		CARGO AND PASSENGER LOADING (CPL)															
CPL	1100	Pass/bag Load Intro	B	A	1	(N*)	*						2.0	1000			
CPL	1101	Pass/bag & Wt and Bal	B,R	A	1	(N*)	*						3.0	1100			
CPL	1102	Rev LM duties to date	B,R	A	1	(N*)	*						3.0	1101			
CPL	1103	Mixed Loading Intro	B,R	A	1	(N*)	*						3.0	1102			
CPL	1104	Pallet & Cargo Load	B,R	A	1	(N*)	*						3.0	1103			
CPL	1105	Pallet Loading Review	B,R	A	1	(N*)	*						3.0	1104			
CPL	1106	Mixed Cargo and Pass	B	A	1	(N*)	*						2.0	1105			
CPL	1107	Progress Review	B,R	A	1	(N*)	*						3.0	1106			
		TOTAL CPL STAGE						0	0.0	0	0.0	8	22.0				
		DISTINGUISHED PASSENGERS (VIP)															
VFAM	1200	Intro VIP Procedures	B	A	1	(N*)	*						2.0	1000			
VFAM	1201	Prac VIP Procedures	B,R	A	1	(N*)	*						2.0	1200			
		TOTAL VIP STAGE						0	0.0	0	0.0	2	4.0				
		TOTAL CORE SKILL INTRODUCTION PHASE (1000 PHASE)						0	0.0	0	0.0	10	26.0				
		CORE SKILL TRAINING (2000 PHASE EVENTS)															
		HAZARDOUS CARGO (HAZFAM)															
HAZFAM	2100	Intro Haz cargo	B	A	1	(N*)	1095	0	0.0	0	0.0	2	2.0	1000, LM School FW JRB			
		TOTAL HAZFAM STAGE						0	0.0	0	0.0	1	2.0				
		TOTAL CORE SKILL PHASE (2000 PHASE)						0	0.0	0	0.0	1	2.0				
		MISSION SKILL TRAINING (3000 PHASE)															
		OPERATIONAL AIRLIFT SUPPORT (OSA)															
OSA	3100	Passenger Mission	B,R,M	A	1	(N*)	180	0	0.0	0	0.0	1	6.0	6200			
		TOTAL OAS STAGE						0	0.0	0	0.0	1	6.0				
		AIR LOGISTICS SUPPORT (ALS)															
ALS	3200	Cargo Mission	B,R,M	A	1	(N*)	180	0	0.0	0	0.0	1	2.0	6200			
		TOTAL ALS STAGE						0	0.0	0	0.0	1	2.0				
		TOTAL MISSION SKILL PHASE (3000 PHASE)						0	0.0	0	0.0	2	8.0				

VMR-1 LOADMASTER T&R MATRIX

STAGE	TRNG CODE	T&R DESCRIMITION	POI	DEVICE E	A/C A	# OF A/C	CON	RE FLY	# OF ACAD	ACAD TIME	# OF SIM	SIM TIME	# OF FLTS	FLT TIME	PREREQUISITE	NOTES	CHAINING	EVENT CONV
		CORE PLUS SKILL TRAINING (4000 PHASE)																
		INTERNATIONAL/TRANS OCEANIC FLIGHTS (IFAM)																
IFAM	4100	Int/Trans O Intro	B		A	1	(N*)	*					3.0	1000			
IFAM	4001	Int/Trans O Rev	B,R,M		A	1	(N*)	365					3.0	4100			
		TOTAL IFAM STAGE											2	6.0				
		MAXIMUM CARGO PROCEDURES (MAXCPL)																
MAXCPL	4200	Max Load Introduction	B		A	1	(N*)	*					3.0	1104			
MAXCPL	4201	Max Load Review	B,R,M		A	1	(N*)	1095					3.0	4200			
		TOTAL MAXCPL STAGE											2	6.0				
		TOTAL CORE PLUS SKILL PHASE (4000 PHASE)							0	0.0	0	0.0	4	12.0				
		TOTAL 1000, 2000, 3000, and 4000 PHASE							0	0.0	0	0.0	15	42.0				
		INSTRUCTOR TRAINING (5000 PHASE EVENTS)																
		INSTRUCTOR UNDER TRAINING (IUT)																
IUT	5100	IMI Eval	B,R	E	A	1	(N*)	*					2.0	6200, 100 hrs in C-9B			
IUT	5101	IME Eval	B,R	E	A	1	(N*)	*					2.0	5100			
IUT	5102	NATOPS I	B,R	E	A	1	(N*)	*					3.0				
		TOTAL IUT STAGE							0	0.0	0	0.0	3	7.0				
		INSTRUCTOR TRAINING (5000 PHASE EVENTS) TOTAL							0	0.0	0	0.0	3	7.0				

Enclosure (1)

VMR-1 LOADMASTER T&R MATRIX

REQUIREMENT, QUALIFICATIONS, AND DESIGNATIONS (RQD) (6000 PHASE)

RQD ACADEMICS (ACAD)

STAGE	TRNG CODE	T&R DESCRIPTION	POI	DEVICE	# OF A/C	CON	RE FLY	# OF ACAD	ACAD TIME	# OF SIM	SIM TIME	# OF FLTS	FLT TIME	PREREQUISITE	NOTES	CHAINING	EVENT CONV
ACAD	6000	NATOPS Open Exam	B,R,M	E			365		5.0								
ACAD	6001	NATOPS Closed Exam	B,R,M	E			365		1.5					6000			
ACAD	6002	NATOPS Oral Exam	B,R,M	E			365		2.0					6000,6001			
ACAD	6005	CRM Ground Class	B,R,M	E			365		2.0								
ACAD	6006	Monthly EP Exam	B,R,M	E			30		1.0								
ACAD	6007	90 EP Practical Rev	B,R,M	E	S/A	1		90		2.0							
TOTAL ACAD STAGE								6	12.5	0	0.3	0	0.0				

NATOPS

STAGE	TRNG CODE	T&R DESCRIPTION	POI	DEVICE	# OF A/C	CON	RE FLY	# OF ACAD	ACAD TIME	# OF SIM	SIM TIME	# OF FLTS	FLT TIME	PREREQUISITE	NOTES	CHAINING	EVENT CONV
NTPS	6100	NATOPS Evaluation	B,R,M	E	A/S	1	(N*)	365					3.0	6000,6001,6002			
NTPS	6101	CRM Flight Evaluation	B,R,M	E	A/S	1	(N*)	365					3.0	6005			
NATOPS TOTAL								0	0.0	0	0.0	2	6.0				

T3P, T2P, TAC DESIGNATIONS (DESG)

STAGE	TRNG CODE	T&R DESCRIPTION	POI	DEVICE	# OF A/C	CON	RE FLY	# OF ACAD	ACAD TIME	# OF SIM	SIM TIME	# OF FLTS	FLT TIME	PREREQUISITE	NOTES	CHAINING	EVENT CONV
DESG	6200	LM Designation Flight	B,R	E	A	1	(N*)	365	0	0.0	0	0.0	1	3.0				
TOTAL DESG STAGE								0	0.0	0	0.0	1	3.0				
RQD TOTAL (6000 PHASE)								6	12.5	0	0.0	3	9.0				
TOTAL 5000,6000 STAGES								6	12.5	0	0.0	6	16.0				

Enclosure (1)